One or Three?

SAARBRÜCKER THEOLOGISCHE FORSCHUNGEN

Herausgegeben von Gotthold Hasenhüttl und Karl-Heinz Ohlig

Band 8

PETER LANG

Frankfurt am Main · Berlin · Bern · Bruxelles · New York · Oxford · Wien

Karl-Heinz Ohlig

One or three?
From the *father of Jesus*
to the trinity

PETER LANG
Europäischer Verlag der Wissenschaften

Bibliographic Information published by Die Deutsche Bibliothek
Die Deutsche Bibliothek lists this publication in the Deutsche Nationalbibliografie; detailed bibliographic data is available in the internet at <http://dnb.ddb.de>.

ISSN 0936-6423
ISBN 3-631-50337-7
US-ISBN 0-8204-6063-X

© Peter Lang GmbH
Europäischer Verlag der Wissenschaften
Frankfurt am Main 2002
All rights reserved.

All parts of this publication are protected by copyright. Any utilisation outside the strict limits of the copyright law, without the permission of the publisher, is forbidden and liable to prosecution. This applies in particular to reproductions, translations, microfilming, and storage and processing in electronic retrieval systems.

www.peterlang.de

Table of Contents

Foreword	9

1. Introduction   11

1.1 A Latent Tritheism   11
1.2 The Reception of the Doctrine of the Trinity in the
    Non-European Churches   16
1.3 Historical-Critical Deficits   19

2. The Pre-Christian Roots   21

2.1 Religious-Historical Analogies to the Trinitarian Conception   21
2.2 The Cultural-Historical Roots of Binitarian and Trinitarian
    Conceptions of God in Early Judaism   23
    2.2.1 Monotheism   23
    2.2.2 The Synthesis of the Biblical God and the Hellenistic God   24
    2.2.3 Binitarian and Trinitarian Conceptions   25
2.3 The End and a New Beginning   29

3. Trinitarian Echoes in the New Testament?   31

3.1 Jesus and God   31
3.2 The New Testament Tradition after Jesus   32
    3.2.1 The Palestinian-Christian and the Diaspora
          Jewish-Christian Tradition   32
    3.2.2 Beginnings of a Hellenistic Christology   34
    3.2.3 Triadic Formulas in the New Testament   35

**4. The Origins of a Christian Doctrine of the Binity or
the Trinity between the 2nd Century and the Beginning
of the 4th Century**   41

4.1 The Theological-Historical Situation   41
    4.1.1 Two New Areas of Activity for God   41
    4.1.2 The Most Significant Cultural Characteristics of the Early
          Christian Church   42
4.2 The Central Variations in the Concept of God until around
    the End of the 2nd Century   43
    4.2.1 Jewish-Christian Traditions   43
    4.2.1.1 The Jewish Profession of Faith in the Monotheistic God   43
    4.2.1.2 The Survival of Early Jewish Angelology   45
4.3 Hellenistic-Christian Traditions   47
    4.3.1 The Profession of Faith in Jesus as „God"   47
    4.3.2 The Development by the Apologists of a Doctrine of the Binity   48

	4.3.3 The Reestablishment of Monotheism by Syrian Theologians	50
	4.3.4 Decisive Impulses from Gnosticism	51
	Example 1: The Odes of Solomon	53
	Example 2: The Valentinian Gnosis	54
	Example 3: The Gospel of the Truth	54
	Example 4: The *Pistis Sophia*	55
4.4	Eternal Monotheism and the „Trinity" in Salvation History	58
4.5	From the Economic to the Eternal Trinity	63
4.6	A Monotheistic Line	66
	4.6.1 Monarchianism and Modalism	66
	4.6.2 The Doctrine of Arius	67

5. The Linguistic Fixing of the Doctrine of the Trinity in the 4th Century — 69

5.1	The Creed of the First Ecumenical Council of Nicaea (325)	69
5.2	The Post-Nicene Development until the Middle of the 4th century	71
	5.2.1 The Conflict over the Interpretation of *homoousios*	71
	5.2.2 The Transition from a Doctrine of the Binity to the Doctrine of the Trinity	74
	5.2.2.1 The Challenge to the Divinity of the Spirit	74
	5.2.2.2 The Acceptance of the Divine Status of the Spirit	74
5.3	The Formula Orthodoxy	77
	5.3.1 One Substance – Three Hypostases	77
	5.3.2 A Latent Tritheism	78
	5.3.3 A Stronger Emphasis on the Unity of God with a Residual „Tritheism"	80
	5.3.4 The Etymological Doctrine of the Trinity	81
5.4	The New Consensus	83

6. The Trinitarian Development in the Latin West — 87

6.1	Trinitarian Disinterest	87
6.2	The Difficulty of the Translation	89
6.3	Augustine's Doctrine of the Trinity	90
	6.3.1 The Taking of the One God as a Starting Point	90
	6.3.2 The Formalized Etymology or the Relational Conception of the Trinity	92
	6.3.3 The (So-called) Psychological Doctrine of the Trinity	95
	6.3.4 The Spirit as Bond of Love	97
6.4	Boethius' Definition of Person	99

7.	**The Consolidation of Western Conceptions of the Trinity in the Middle Ages**	103
7.1	The Safety of Formulaic Language and the Victory of the Trinitarian Etymology	103
7.2	The „Three – I-Don't-Know-Whats" or the Interest in the One God	105
7.3	The Threefold Community of Love	108
	7.3.1 Three Self-Conscious Persons in God	108
	7.3.2 The „Exultation in Selfless Love"	111
7.4	Excursus: The Triadic Self-Fulfillment of God	114
8.	**Nothing New Since the Middle Ages**	119
9.	**From Monotheism to the Intradivine Community of Love**	121
9.1	The Contextual Limitation of the Trinitarian Dogma	121
	9.1.1 Cultural-Historical Inevitabilities	122
	9.1.2 Two Historical „Accidents" and their Impact	127
9.2	A Religious Studies Résumé and a Theological Question	128
List of Abbreviation		131
Bibliography		133

Foreword

The intention of the following study is to explain how it was that Trinitarian ideas could in the course of a few centuries become connected with the one God of Israel and Father of Jesus. It makes no claim to reproduce the entire history of the doctrine of the Trinity; it will be limited to the time period from the doctrine's beginnings to the consolidation of its central formulation – in the fourth century in the Eastern Church and at the time of the early Scholastics in Western theology.

All further designs on the theme of the Trinity are based on these terminological agreements and hence no longer contribute to them per se, but merely interpret them in each case within new contexts and from highly personal points of view. As interesting as it may be to familiarize oneself with the more exact Trinitarian ideas of *Thomas Aquinas*, *Luther*, *Hegel* or *Schleiermacher*, their ideas are of little import for the history of the Trinity itself, the results of which they assume.

Just as little is it a question here of a thorough analysis of all the Biblical material or of the Trinity concepts of individual theologians, such as *Justinian*, *Origen*, *Tertullian* or *Augustine*. They will only be referred to insofar as it can be established that they have taken new steps in the direction of the fixing of the Trinitarian formula and later normative motifs. Those who have further questions are invited to refer to the adequately available literature on the subject.

The way, however, in which the monotheism accompanying Christianity was corrected by Trinitarian ideas will in this study be documented by source material in such a way that the reader can *follow* the course of development and *form his or her own opinion*. It is not a question of adding to the countless interpretations yet another, that of the present writer. History itself should get a word in, so that the individual stages and the particular motivations will become visible.

For the sake of legibility the use of Greek and Latin original texts has for the most part been avoided and for the English translation reference has been made to easily accessible editions in which, in turn, more exact notes are to be found. The secondary literature will also only be referred to insofar as it contributes directly to the presentation; a comprehensive discussion of the abundant literature will not be undertaken.

1. Introduction[1]

1.1 A Latent Tritheism

„Trinity"[2] is the name given to the doctrine, developed in the early Christian era, of the *one* God who is at the same time „Father," „Son" and „Holy Spirit" and thus triadic – in three hypostases or persons – without losing through this trinity His unity and simplicity.
No Trinitarian ideas occur in the New Testament. Instead, they first evolved in the course of second century when older patterns were taken over from early Judaism and reinforced – especially in the context of a development of the Christological dual-nature doctrine.
In the year 325 the first „doctrinal" milestone was laid by the First Ecumenical Council of Nicea which defined the substantial identity of the „Son" with the Father; the second ecumenical council, the first of Constantinople in the year 381, also predicated divinity of the „Holy Spirit."
The terminological description of the Trinity still used today stems from the second half of the fourth century when the bishop and theologian *Basil* of Caesarea created the formula of the one essence (ousia) in three hypostases. Several centuries later this was translated in the West by the expression of one *essentia* and three *personae*.
Ever since the first great councils of Christian antiquity, the declaration of one's belief in the one Trinitarian God or in God the Father, Son and Holy Spirit has been considered to be a central or, indeed, *the* central article of faith; the Trinity has been considered to be the means of the self-revelation of God, and its exposition and the reflection on it has been considered to be the most difficult task of theology, which here comes up against the limits of what can be humanly thought or expressed.
Official ecclesiastical writers consider their documents especially well-wrought if they have a „Trinitarian" structure, for example, the adult catechism published by the German bishops[3] or the universal catechism.[4] *Karl Rahner*'s

---

[1] This study is the revised version of an article series entitled „Einer oder drei? Vom ‚Vater Jesu' zur Trinität" in the journal *imprimatur* (No. 29, 1996, 285-91; 340-46; No. 30, 1997, 8-13; 55-59; 108-11; 147-52; 199-204; 315-23; No. 31, 1998, 18-27; 74-80; 174-80 ff.); it was also published in German in a greatly reduced form under the title „Ein Gott in drei Personen. Die griechische Komplizierung des jüdischen Monotheismus" in a collection of essays edited by Rudolf Laufen, Düsseldorf, on dual-nature and preexistence Christology, *Gottes ewiger Sohn. Die Präexistenz Christi* (Paderborn, München, Wien, Zürich, 1997), pp. 199-226.
[2] The Greek term on which it was based, „Trias," was first used by Theophilos of Antioch (second half of the second century) in *ad Autol.* II 15.
[3] *Katholischer Erwachsenen-Katechismus. Das Glaubensbekenntnis der Kirche*, ed. Deutsche Bischofskonferenz (Kevelaer, etc., 1985).
[4] *Katechismus der Katholischer Kirche* (München, etc., 1993).

complaint that a treatise on the Trinity, once it has been treated in a piece of dogmatics, never appears again,[5] no longer seems true, at least at the present time; rather it must be feared that an abundance of (mostly inappropriate) topics are being interpreted in a directly Trinitarian manner – which is only possible with excessive speculation that is dangerous for the identity of Christianity.[6] For then it is possible to treat the family, the structure of human thought or of the psyche, and even High Mass from a Trinitarian perspective. *Gerhard Ebeling* calls such a procedure „a logical abstraction from the experience and a distancing of oneself from the situation of the disputed faith, a godless playing-out of divine structures and a confounding of the perfection of God with theological perfection."[7]

In a bizarre way the Trinity dogma seems to have been spared the consequences of a historical critique. As in the days of Scholasticism and of orthodoxies in all their versions, the Old Church definitions are treated as if they were not open to analysis, but are merely to be „postulated" in a positivistic way and then deepened systematically with the understanding. Not even the well-known results of the exegesis of the New Testament since the Age of Enlightenment have aroused the suspicion of Trinity theologians; on the contrary, they often interpret the New Testament on the basis of the later dogmas. Similarly, the countless and often quite thorough studies in the history of the development of the Trinitarian dogma have apparently still not moved them even to ask questions. Developments, leaps, ruptures are all harmoniously interpreted from the point of view of the results (apparently) established with Nicaea and the First Council of Constantinople, with *Basil* or *Augustine*.

In any case, it can be observed that almost all of the more renowned theologians of this century and above all of recent times take as a starting point the dogma that the Christian God is *one in three persons*. They differ from one another in that in some of them a certain embarrassment can be sensed with respect to the number three, whereas others emphasize it in such an uninhibited way that for all intents and purposes one would have to speak of a tritheism, albeit of one occurring within *one* entity, i.e., of a belief in three gods. They further differ in the choice of contexts for the description as far as the „content" is concerned of that which in the doctrine of the Trinity is to be understood under „person." Thus, for example, *Karl Rahner* wants to make a sharp distinction between the Trinitarian and the „modern" concept of person

---

[5] Bemerkungen zum dogmatischen Traktat „De Trinitate", in *Schriften zur Theologie, Bd. IV: Neuere Schriften* (Zürich/Einsiedeln/Köln, 1960), p. 108.

[6] A two-volume bibliography extending from antiquity to the time of its going to press (*Bibliotheca Trinitariorum. Internationale Bibliographie trinitarisher Literatur. International Trinitarian Literature*, ed. Erwin Schadel [Paris, München, New York, (Vol. 1) 1984, (Vol. 2) 1988]) contains 5,679 titles; moreover, since that time, by my count, more than 200 items have been published.

[7] *Dogmatik des christlichen Glaubens*, Vol. III: *Der Glaube an Gott den Vollender der Welt* (Tübingen, 1979), p. 540.

and refers more emphatically back to the – because of its formality more harmless – concept of subsistence, derived from late classical theology.[8] *Rahner*'s proposed formulation of the „three ways of subsistence" in God[9] thus attempts to avoid the misunderstanding of a trio of „I's" in God, yet suggests a real trinity in God; the conception also presents itself as a résumé of the rest of *Rahner*'s theology, above all in what he says specifically about Father, Son and Holy Spirit.

Karl Barth also has certain reservations concerning the concept of person and occasionally speaks of the three ways of being[10] of the one God. Thus at least the Creation (though not the Incarnation) would be a work of the entire Trinity.[11] Nevertheless, it goes without saying that he takes as his starting point the Old Church formulations („As the Father God in eternity creates Himself in His Son, and He is also with His Son from all eternity the origin of Himself in the Holy Spirit"[12]), interprets New Testament texts on the basis of them and even includes the man Jesus in the eternal Trinitarian events in a highly contestable manner.

Bernd Jochen Hilberath in his book *Der dreieinige Gott und die Gemeinschaft der Menschen: Orientierungen zur christlichen Rede von Gott*[13] expresses the problems involved in applying the concept of a person to God. If person in the sense of *Boethius* is used in the doctrine of the Trinity, the doctrine would be exposed „to the risk of tritheism, of the belief in three gods."[14] However, he likewise rejects talk of God's three ways of manifesting Himself or of being, since then one would run „the other risk, that of modalism."[15] He himself wants instead to take up newer currents of thought according to which „person" only comes into existence in the encounter with a „Thou." „A human being only becomes a person in community with a person."[16]

That sounds fine, but it leads nowhere. How, in the case of God, would it be possible to think that His persons first „come to be"? This is just as aporetic as

---

[8] This theology had increasingly come to feel that the at first commonly employed translation of the Greek word for that which is triple in God (*hypostasis*, „hypostasis," literally: a standing under) by the Latin term *substantia* („substance," a standing under) was inappropriate and replaced it with the actually synonymous but more rarely used term of *subsistentia* („subsistence," a standing under).

[9] „Einzigkeit und Dreifaltigkeit Gottes im Gespräch mit dem Islam" in *Schriften zur Theologie*, Vol. XIII: *Gott und Offenbarung* (Zürich, Einsiedeln, Köln, 1978), p. 138.

[10] *Kirchliche Dogmatik*, Vol III/1: *Die Lehre von der Schöpfung* (Zürich, ³1957), p. 52.

[11] Ibid., p. 51 ff.

[12] *Kirchliche Dogmatik*, loc. cit., p. 52.

[13] *Der dreieinige Gott und die Gemeinschaft der Menschen: Orientierungen zur christlichen Rede von Gott* (Mainz, 1990), pp. 33-4.

[14] *Der dreieinige Gott und die Gemeinschaft der Menschen*, loc. cit., p. 33.

[15] Ibid.

[16] Ibid.

the contrary formulation: God first becomes one through the community of previously existing persons.
The relative Trinitarian moderation of *Barth* and *Rahner* (but also that, among others, of *Gerhart Ebeling* or *Wilfried Joest*) is not followed by many. For *Wolfhart Pannenberg* there has been from all eternity an „inner-godly opposition of Father and Son." „The being of God, as it is revealed in the life of Christ, thus has in itself the duality, the tension and the relationship in Father and Son"[17] (and probably Holy Spirit too); the unity and singularity of God seems thereby to have been abandoned. *Jürgen Moltmann* even sees the Trinity as originating „out of the interaction of the three divine subjects."[18] Here, in the book *Trinität und Reich Gottes*, the three subjects are „conceived of as separate centers of consciousness, will and action."[19] Depending on the subject, *Moltmann* keeps up this concept even in passages that appear to treat the concept of person with more moderation.[20] He therefore imagines God to be more like an additive unity of three subjects.
In his text *In der Geschichte des dreieinigen Gottes: Beiträge zur trinitarischen Theologie*, he writes: „In my Trinitarian theology I have taken as my starting point the story of Christ from the Bible and thus the difference and the community of the subjects: *Jesus*, the messianic Son, the *Abba-God* invoked by Him and the Holy Ghost, which links Jesus with the Father and comes to the world through him. If one takes the Trinitarian story of the three subjects as one's starting point, then one must inquire about these three subjects in the story of Christ from the Bible and conceive of them in a Trinitarian way, and not in a monistic [monotheistic? K.-H. O.] way. I have then interpreted the unity of Jesus the Son with the Father according to the Gospel of St. John as a *perichoretic unity*, i.e., as a social unity of ‚I' and ‚Thou' in the ‚We' and ‚Us,' in the reciprocal give and take, and in communicating as well as participating life. The term *perichoresis*, the *circuminsessio*, which was introduced into the doctrine of the Trinity by John of Damascus, best grasps the unity of the three persons. Through their reciprocal love they exist in one another in perfect empathy so that they are totally one. In the intensive exchange of their energy they interpenetrate one another perfectly and communicate themselves to one another totally."[21]
Moltmann himself writes that with this view monotheism is in the end abolished and he assesses that – incomprehensibly – as positive. Even if one considers – as mitigating factors – that his aim is to criticize, along the lines

---

[17] *Grundzüge der Christologie* (Gütersloh, ⁵1976), p. 160.
[18] *Trinität und Reich Gottes* (Munich, 1980), p. 110; cf. pp. 146-7.
[19] Regina Radlbeck-Ossmann, „... in drei Personen: Der trinitarische Schlüsselbegriff ‚Person' in den Entwürfen Jürgen Moltmanns und Walter Kaspers (Prof. Dr. W. Beinert zum 60. Geburtstag)" in *Catholica* 47 (1993), p. 40.
[20] Cf. R. Radlbeck-Ossmann, loc. cit., pp 38-44.
[21] *In der Geschichte des dreieinigen Gottes: Beiträge zur trinitarischen Theologie* (München, 1991), p. 181.

of feminist theology, the traditional patriarchal image of God, his formulations are insupportable for Christians, who, together with Jews and Moslems, count themselves among the monotheists. He praises, for example, „the orthodox dogmatic tradition that took the Trinity seriously and defended it against every threat of monotheism."[22] In another book he similarly claims: „Wherever the religion of a patriarchal society has predominated, there arose a religious tendency toward *monotheism* and a political tendency toward the development of monarchist rule."[23] This claim is at least incorrect for the *origin* of monotheism; it is rather the case that wherever there is patriarchy there is *poly*theism (and even the *monisms* of the Far Eastern world religions were formed in patriarchal societies); it was in a social framework under *foreign rule* that *monotheism* arose (Jews in exile under Babylonian rule) and was cultivated (under Persian, Hellenistic, then Roman rule).

Among contemporary theologians *Jürgen Moltmann* – and his conscious follower on the Catholic side, *Gisbert Greshake*[24] – is the one who has succumbed the most to the danger of tritheism inherent in the doctrine of the Trinity („Monotheism is heresy" is one of *Moltmann*'s statements cited by *Luise Abramowski*[25]). With his consciously anti-monotheistic polemic, however, he has only clearly articulated what for many theologians is supposed to be concealed – often behind verbal mumbo jumbo – not just from others, but also from themselves, namely the endangerment of monotheism. As long as one holds on to a real, tendentially subjective (or in modern terms „personal") trinity in God, the danger of the loss of monotheism exists. It is of no use – as *Walter Kasper*, for example, has done – to try to understand the concept of subject or person „relationally" in (conceptual) imitation of *Augustine*, that is (actually against *St. Augustine*) in relation to the other subject,[26] or – following *Regina Radlbeck-Ossmann*'s suggestion – in the sense of a „dialogical personalism."[27] As long as behind all the clever interpretations and qualifications there nevertheless appears a trinity which is conceived of as real, monotheism – there is no getting around it – is threatened or has already been abandoned. Of course it is verbally retained by the vast majority of theologians, insofar as they enthusiastically profess their faith in the one and even the single God. But what does such a declaration of faith still entail if Father, Son and Holy Spirit are nevertheless really different?

---

[22] *Trinität und Reich Gottes*, loc. cit., p. 181.

[23] Cf. „In der Geschichte des dreieinigen Gottes," loc. cit., p. 29.

[24] Gisbert Greshake, *Der dreieine Gott: Eine trinitarische Theologie* (Freiburg, Basel, Wien, 1997); cf. my review, „Spekulation ohne historische Basis," in *imprimatur* 30, 1997, pp. 18-21.

[25] „Zur Trinitätslehre des Thomas von Aquin" in *Zeitschrift für Theologie und Kirche* 92, 1995, p. 471.

[26] Cf., for example, R. Radlbeck-Ossmann, loc. cit., pp. 44-49.

[27] Ibid., p. 51.

The conventional answer to such objections is a reference to the *mysterious nature* of the doctrine of the Trinity. *This* revelation of God concerning his reality is simply inaccessible to human understanding, a mystery in the true sense of the word, and the paradox of unity and trinity is to be accepted on faith and precisely without being understood; any attempt at an adequate explanation is in itself already *hubris* and unbelief.

What would be the case, however, if a glance at the actual history of Trinitarian dogma were to demonstrate that the triadic structuring of the concept of God has borne within it a thoroughly human, and in all of its stages, understandable and logical causality? What would be the case if not divine revelation, but the peculiar progress of the history of human reflection had created the Trinitarian concept? In any event, one should be careful not to introduce the topos of mystery all too early in the debate. Not every aporia is a sign of numinous incomprehensibility.

1.2 The Reception of the Doctrine of the Trinity in the Non-European Churches

The theologies outside of Europe also run the risk of all too quickly appropriating the testimony of the European doctrine of the Trinity in order by means of this pattern – which, because of missionary history, they consider to be unquestionable – to give expression to their own concerns. In Latin America, Asia and Africa, the Trinitarian conception is being used to justify and convey ideas of one's own.

Liberation theology in Latin America sees in the Trinity the eternal foundation of the standard Christian idea of a necessary social solidarity. *Leonardo Boff* – who will here stand typologically for an entire direction of thought which of course includes other variations – summarizes the views of liberation theology in his book *Kleine Trinitätslehre*.[28] The first of its ten chapters is entitled „In the beginning is the community of the Three and not the solitude of the one." The first subsections are „1. From the solitude of the One to the community of the Three" and „2. In the beginning is the community." Here the tendency to ground the demanded social solidarity in the eternal being of God becomes clear: God is from all eternity – consistent with liberation theology and its emphasis on the notion of community – a united community of three subjects. Thus *Boff* writes: „We believe that God is not solitude, but community. It is not the One that comes first, but the Three. First comes the Three. Only then, on the basis of the close relationship among the Three, does the One come – as the expression of the unity of the Three. Believing in the Trinity means assuming that truth and community are mutually interdependent and not mutually exclusive, that consensus expresses the truth better than getting one's way. ... Human existence is never mere life, but always living together. ...

---

[28] L. Boff, *Kleine Trinitätslehre* (Düsseldorf, 1990).

Therefore we should not hesitate in our belief in the social mode of existence of God, in the triune substance of God that is always community and unity of three."[29] Any harmonious pantheon of a polytheism could base itself upon propositions such as these.

Indian Christianity is currently intensively taking up precisely the Trinitarian statements about God. In them are seen the strongest correspondence between Christian doctrine and their own tradition. The latter has indeed recognized a series of triadic divinities. Here, for example, one could cite the development since the beginning of the Christian era of the Hinduistic doctrine of a „*Trimurti*" according to which *God* is *a unity made up of Brahman, Vishnu and Shiva*. Even more important is the Indian theological tradition of doing without any reference to myths of the gods. According to this tradition God is not thought of as personal, but as material: he is the first principle and ultimate reality of the world; the visible cosmos is „God's body," i.e., the material manifestation of the divine being. In India this material-divine reality has from time immemorial been conceived of triadically and been described by the formula „saccidanandam" (from „sat-cit-ananda": „sat" = being, „cit" = consciousness, and „ananda" = bliss).

This old notion is combined with or even assimilated to the Christian doctrine of the Trinity by Indo-Christian theology. Father, Son and Spirit here appear as the mythical (because „personalized") forms of the triadic material God. This combination was first produced by *Keshab Chandra Sen* († 1884). Since that time it has been taken up again and again, most recently and perhaps most dramatically by the Jesuit *Francis X. D'Sa* in his article: „God – Person or Principle? The Concept of God in the Development of Indian Theology."[30]

That which in the formula appears to suggest total agreement with the European Christian tradition in fact aims at a new, at a different understanding of God. In any event the problem seems to lie less in a latent tritheism – the three versions of God are after all only different aspects of *our* reflection of the *one* divine being – than in a fundamentally monistic thinking of God.

The situation in *Africa*, on the other hand, is a different one. There in the vast majority of the forms of Christianity (of all confessions) theology is practiced in connection with the European mother church, orders, missionary societies, confessions, etc.; it is thus a question of reproductions of European Western theology. At the same time, however, there is a constantly increasing awareness of one's own religious tradition on the basis of whose patterns the Christian doctrine is reflected and its practice Africanized.

For our concerns the different expressions of the supernatural world from one tribe to another do not play a major role. In that world the people are closest to the deceased *ancestors* who at first continue – usually for five generations – to intervene in the destinies of their descendants – almost as if they were still

---

[29] L. Boff, *Kleine Trinitätslehre*, ibid. p. 15.

[30] In: K. Hilpert and K.-H. Ohlig, eds., *Der eine Gott in vielen Kulturen: Inkulturation und christliche Gottesvorstellung* (Zürich, 1993), pp. 169-200.

alive: one speaks of the „living dead." After this phase they turn into *spirits* who to a certain extent lose their individuality and achieve a state of collective immortality, but in which they are still numinous powers. Standing over them there are usually (not in all tribes), and sometimes in addition to natural spirits, a more or less large number of gods, and above them all there is the *one* God who created everything.

The fundamental structure of this whole system was first identified by a Belgian missionary named *Placide Tempels*, whose book *Bantou-Filosofie* was published in 1955[31]; virtually all contemporary theologians and divinity scholars draw upon his theses. According to him, the all-controlling idea of a *„force vitale,"* of a vital force, stands at the center of black African religiosity, a vital force which from out of itself produces biological and, at the same time, spiritual life. The one God of creation is in this thinking the *origin of all life force*, which He passes on to all mankind and to the entire universe by way of the gods and above all the ancestral spirits.

In Christian theology these interpretational frameworks are applied to the Trinity, for example, by *Bénézet Bujo*: „The Father, who possesses an infinite life force, creates the Son, and both live for one another; they live in this way in a large and total, vital union which mutually reinforces this community of life: The life force which emanates from the Father to the Son and creates Him, returns from the latter to the Father. ... This vital union, which leads to the interaction between the Father and the Son and in this way constitutes the bond between the two, is nothing but the divine force which, because it is internal to God, is a concrete gestalt and can be equated with the Holy Spirit. ..."[32]

Bujo believes – and this is an old point of contention between us – that without a doubt the African pre-Christian conceptions of God represented a *monotheism*.[33] In my view, however, this is not the case. Monotheism includes as its core the radicalization of the thought of the person all the way to the god who – like Yahweh – in the Hebrew language does not even have a generic name „god," but is only addressed with a proper name.

At the core of the African conception of god, however, is the „vital force," i.e., a primarily biological and, hence, *material* force. Thus this can also – without problem – diversify itself plurally, and there is likewise no reason why it could not be specified again in one and the same God since one can think of *forces* being multiplied without suspending the unity (cf. the variegated forms of what in the end is just *one* nature); the person of God, however, cannot be multiplied without creating a polytheism.

This is also why the Africanization of European Trinitarian conceptions, as proposed by *Bujo*, results *not in a tritheism* (although it may sometimes sound

---

[31] „*Bantu-Philosophie*": *Ontologie einer Ethik* (title of the original Belgian edition: *Bantou-Filosofie*), German translation by Joseph Peters (Heidelberg, 1956).

[32] *Afrikanische Theologie in ihrem gesellschaftlichen Kontext* (Düsseldorf, 1986), p. 92.

[33] Loc. cit., p. 22.

like it when, in addition, he employs linguistic models taken from liberation theology), but rather more typically in a *latent monism* in so far as the attempt is made to think God under the main idea of a material *force vitale*.

Thus in Asian and African theologies the Trinitarian formula has been taken up with much approval, often even with enthusiasm. Here, however, the trinity has been superseded by and preserved in fundamentally monistic structures, so that it is *not the trinity* but the *impersonal or transpersonal* concept of God that makes a problem out of monotheism.

In Africa, though, the monism does not appear to be of such a reflected and systematic sort as is the case, for example, in India; it can therefore be more easily and inconspicuously combined with Christian-personal conceptions. In an overview of the current situation in the theological Trinitarian discussion, it thus becomes evident that *in – in the broadest sense of the term – „Western" and liberation theology the threat to monotheism is latently or openly tritheistic, whereas in Asia and Africa the threat to monotheism is monistic.*

1.3 Historical-Critical Deficits

All traditions, however, quite naturally take as their starting point the dogmatic formulations of the early Church. Historical-critical formulations of the question are at best taken up in propaedeutical areas and are not seriously analyzed with respect to their impact on an understanding of the belief in the Trinity. Oddly enough, it is hardly ever asked how it came about that the inherited Jewish monotheism, which Jesus of Nazareth doubtless shared, was changed in Christianity into a Trinitarian conception, why and with what right Christianity has departed from the – nevertheless allegedly normative – understanding of God of Jesus and „the twelve Apostles."

It is indeed often complained that – because of its complexity – the vast majority of Christians are only very deficiently informed about the doctrine of the Trinity. A part of the Christians live, without contesting the dogma, as if God were unitarily One, but most of them are probably closet tritheists.[34] Admittedly, if asked, they would passionately underscore their faith in the one God, but in practice they turn, in their prayers, depending on the situation, to the Father, Son or Spirit as if to three different addressees or subjects.

Numerous supports are also provided for this by the ecclesiastical liturgies of all confessions to the extent that, although their prayers are usually directed to God the Father, they also quite frequently address the Son and the Spirit. To be sure, historians of the liturgy know that this is a relatively late development

---

[34] Karl Rahner, „Einigkeit und Dreifaltigkeit Gottes im Gespräch mit Islam" in *Schriften zur Theologie XIII: Gott und Offenbarung* (Zürich, Einsiedeln, Köln, 1978), p. 147; by the same author, „Der dreifaltige Gott als transzendenter Urgrund der Heilsgeschichte" in *Mysterium Salutis: Grundriß heilsgeschichtlicher Dogmatik*, eds. J. Feiner and M. Löhrer, Vol. II: *Die Heilsgeschicht vor Christus* (Einsiedeln, Zürich, Köln, 1967), pp. 319-323.

and that it was only gradually that the classical prayer to the Father and the Son and the Holy Ghost – as all orations in the Catholic Mass which stem from the time of the early Church still conclude today – was replaced by prayers to one or the other of the three persons; however, they have not drawn any corrective consequences from this knowledge.

To be examined in the following chapters are where the roots of the Trinitarian modification of monotheism are to be found, what the motives were that played a role in it, which developments and upheavals can be identified and what the significance of all this is for an understanding of the doctrine of the Trinity. It will not be a question here of countering the traditional doctrine with a personal opinion – like an antithesis to a thesis – but rather the historical sources will be allowed to speak for themselves and to show us the way to an *understanding*.

2. The Pre-Christian Roots

2.1 Religious-Historical Analogies to the Trinitarian Conception[35]

In very many religions there are triads of gods or even triadic structures of the divinity – usually at the top of the pantheon. This is also true for the religious milieu of Israel and early Christianity. The causalities active in this connection as well as their possible impact on the development of the Judeo-Christian conceptions will only be mentioned here, but will not be more closely examined.[36] It should suffice to indicate that in these contexts it was at least not unusual, and was perhaps even encouraged, to associate with God the number three.

Early forms of the connection of the number three with the realm of the divine can be found all around the world and already very early on in the religious forms of prehistory[37]; besides other number symbolisms (as far as the duality, quaternary, octonary, etc. are concerned) triads (trinities of gods, triformed or three-headed dieties, three-in-one trinities) then played a special role in early advanced civilizations.

A few examples should be sufficient: In the Sumerian religion the three gods An (heaven), Emlil (storm) and Enki (ground water) stand at the top of the pantheon; this cosmic triad was taken over in the Babylonian-Assyrian culture (under the names of Anu, Ellil or Bel/Ea), to which was added an astral trio consisting of Sin (the moon god), Shamash (the sun god) and Ishtar (the morning and evening star). In the Egyptian religion there is the trinity of Osiris, Isis and Horus, as well as the nonity of gods (three times three = the

---

[35] Cf. by the present author „Trinity" in *Lexikon Alte Kulturen*, eds. H. Brunner, K. Flessel, F. Hiller and Meyer's Lexicon Editorial Staff (Mannheim, Leipzig, Wien, Zürich, 1993), pp. 559-560.

[36] Cf., for example, Peter Gerlitz, *Außerchristliche Einflüsse auf die Entwicklung des christlichen Trinitätsdogmas* (Leiden, 1963).

[37] „Triadic motifs" are already found in the Neopaleolithic period (40,000 to 10,000 B.C.), in the phase of human history from which for the first time religious documents in greater numbers have been preserved. *Louis-René Nougier, Die Welt der Höhlenmenschen* (French original: *Premiers éveils de l'homme* [Paris 1984], trans. Verena E. Müller (Zürich, München, 1989) recognizes numinous trinities in the representations occasionally to be found at the entrances of the decorated caves of father animal, mother animal and young animal that appear to be striding out of the cave. „I would like to call these families with their supplementary cosmogonic significance the ‚creative trinity' which climbs out of the subterranean depths" (ibid. p. 246). These triadic patterns then seem to be more strongly mirrored in symbols that obviously possess sacred and numinous connotations and which appeared at the same time and soon began to occur more frequently: triangles with and without a point in the middle, as well as the – repeatedly appearing – three lines or three points drawn on the walls of Early Stone Age cult buildings in the Near East, or etched onto menhirs of the Neolithic megalithic culture or into Bronze Age cult utensils.

totality) of On/Heliopolis. The ancient Roman religion recognizes the trinity of Jupiter-Mars-Quirinus, later replaced by the Capitoline triad of Jupiter-Juno-Minerva. In the oldest Vedic era (Rigveda) three sons of Prjapati, the Lord of Creation, steer the entire universe (Agni = fire, Vayu = wind and Surya = sun); in the post-Vedic era the *trimurti* (Sanskrit: triform) of Brahma (the universal god), Vishnu (the „preserver") and „Shiva" (the „destroyer") comes to the fore, next to it both the triad of the syllable Om (a-u-m) and the Brahman as the unity of being, consciousness and happiness[38] have been meditated. Also, Buddhism (especially Mahayana Buddhism), Parseeism, and numerous other religions recognize triadic structures.

There are, in addition to a religious-psychological affinity to the trinity, clearly other motives for dividing up the central sphere of the divine in this way. Included among them is the threefold structure of the cosmos in the prescientific world view (earth, heaven, underworld), the core both of the family (father, mother, child) and of a group (*tres faciunt collegium*), the trinity of birth, life, death, etc. Perhaps there is a „triadic structural principle of reality" that in the end deepened itself „into a Trinitarian understanding of God."[39] Beyond the concept of God, in many religions a preference for threefold series can also be established in other connections.

In *Greek and even more so in Hellenistic philosophy* (Platonism, especially Neoplatonism, stoicism, etc.) the notion of a duality or trinity of the divine plays an even greater role: All variety in the cosmos originated in *one* final inner cause or *one* immanent principle of the world out of which everything has proceeded and which is active in everything (Hellenistic monism). The more this original principle was reflected upon, the more clearly it was looked upon as being *one, simple and unchanging* that would lose its simplicity and immutability through an action (e.g., the creation of the world). For this reason, a *second principle* was postulated, itself divine, but of a lower rank, proceeding in passive emanation from the first principle, which could take over the task of creating the world (demiurge [world creator], *logos* [word] or *nous* [spirit]); in many directions of thought even this second principle was considered to be so far from all plurality that it itself could still not constitute the world deep down, so that for this purpose a *third principle* that immanently constitutes the cosmos had to be taken up (as, for example, in Neoplatonism, where the realm of the divine is divided into three parts: [1] the one [Greek: *to hen*], so singularly *one* that it can bear in itself no determination at all, not even being; [2] the spirit [Greek: *ho nous*], the epitome of Plato's ideal world; and [3] the world soul [Greek: *he psychê*]).

---

[38] Cf. Introduction above, p. 17.

[39] As suggested by Heinrich Beck, „Triadische Götterordnungen: klassisch-antiker und neuplatonischer Ansatz" in *Theologie und Philosophie* 67, 1992, p. 230.

2.2 The Cultural-Historical Roots of Binitarian and Trinitarian Conceptions of God in Early Judaism

2.2.1 Monotheism

In the 7th/6th century B.C. the Jewish religion produced from more ancient roots the theoretical monotheism whose concern was the universal power and validity of Yahweh. According to the findings of recent research, which does not from the outset „explain away" alternative traditions in terms of the eventually victorious monotheistic position, polytheistic conceptions nevertheless still continued to have an effect that certainly also favored the later binitarian development. „The old polytheism of Israel even left a number of traces in strictly monotheistic texts. Occasionally the different gods of the polytheism simply flow together and are only still identifiable to the sharp eye of the historian of religion," writes *Bernhard Lang*.[40] He points to Prov. 1-9 where Yahweh „is encountered alternately in the role of the Creator God Elohim ... and the local god,"[41] to Deut. 32.8f. LXX with the parallel appearance of the more powerful El Elyon and Yahweh (see also Prov. 30.4),[42] to Dan. 7, in which an older god passes the power „to a younger god" – „The young god is designated as the Son of Man"[43] – as well as to „Lady Wisdom" in the wisdom books.[44]

In principle, however, and with an increasingly polemical emphasis, monotheism stood at the center of Jewish piety and theology and was also shared by Jesus. Although there was still then a certain differentiation between God himself (Yahweh) and his action in history and the cosmos („word of Yahweh," „spirit of Yahweh," „wisdom of Yahweh"), this differentiation remained fundamentally integrated in the unity of Yahweh and had only a functional significance, so that the monotheism was preserved. What therefore needs to be explained is why, in the early Judaism of the second and first pre-Christian centuries,[45] in the late texts of the New Testament and – with a vengeance – in Christian theology since the second century, this firm monotheism was supplemented, corrected, and „enriched" by plural elements.

---

[40] Bernhard Lang, „Der monarchische Monotheismus und die Konstellation zweier Götter im Frühjudentum: Ein neuer Versuch über Menschensohn, Sophia und Christologie," in *Ein Gott allein? JHWH-Verehrung und biblischer Monotheismus im Kontext der israelitischen und altorientalischen Religionsgeschichte*, eds. Walter Dietrich and Martin A. Klopfenstein (*Orbis biblicus et orientalis* 139), (Göttingen, Freiburg [Switzerland], 1994), p. 560.
[41] Ibid.
[42] Ibid.
[43] Ibid., p. 561.
[44] Ibid., p. 562.
[45] Cf. Gottfried Schimanowski, „Die frühjüdischen Voraussetzungen der urchristlichen Präexistenzchristologie," in *Gottes ewiger Sohn*, loc. cit., pp. 31-55.

2.2.2 The Synthesis of the Biblical God and the Hellenistic God

This took place in contexts in which early Judaism was defined by Hellenistic influences; in Jesus himself and in a large part of the New Testament their impact can be estimated to have been less.[46] Alone this rather superficial observation may already indicate what through a more precise analysis will become a certainty: *Binitarian and Trinitarian ideas were formed where Jewish monotheism and Hellenistic conceptions of god came together*, where Jewish historical orientation and Hellenistic cosmos-centristic thinking, where the Jewish and the Hellenistic manner of formulating and answering the question of meaning, hence where these two soteriological forms[47] entered into contact with one another. In the first „case" god is conceived of as being the beginning and the end of history and as being its current king and lord, who, acting in the manner of a person, deliberately intervenes in the ways in which it proceeds. In short, Yahweh is the *god of history*; and just as a human subject stands opposite others and the world − transcending them − so also is Yahweh imagined according to this model. He is absolutely transcendent to the world and history and is „the completely other" without any natural connection with the creature.

The Hellenistic conception of god is completely different: here god is *the innermost and ultimate basis of the cosmos* and of all cosmic being. He is an impersonal principle, and hence incapable of acting, or the one (passive) cause (*aitía*) of everything; he is *in* everything so that everything is also divine (a latently or openly monistic conception). Nevertheless, this god is not simply identical with the cosmos and its colorful variety since, after all, he is its *one* basis. He is therefore transcendent with regard to the plurality of the visible world, although in ultimate causality he is simultaneously also its being. This transcendence of the *world* is completely different from Yahweh's transcendence of *history*.[48]

Early Judaism knew two different cultural expressions. In Palestine itself, despite being a part of the extended Hellenistic area, its own, especially apocalyptic traditions were more determining than in Diaspora Judaism, which was more strongly Hellenized. The beginnings of the Jewish Diaspora date back in Mesopotamia to the 8th century, in Egypt to the beginning of the 6th century. Especially in Lower Egypt, but also on the upper course of the Nile

---

[46] Although the editorship of the writings of the New Testament was as a rule (probably even exclusively) due to *Hellenized* Jewish Christians, an important part, e.g. the Synoptic Gospels, is indeed − toward *Luke* to an increasing extent − characterized by Hellenistic motifs; nevertheless in them the fundamental „salvation-history" pattern of all religious interpretation, in the manner characteristic of Jewish thinking, is not abandoned.

[47] Cf. by the present author, *Fundamentalchristologie. Im Spannungsfeld von Christentum und Kultur* (München, 1986), Pts. I and II, pp. 19-306, passim.

[48] Cf. by the present author, *Die Welt ist Gottes Schöpfung. Kosmos und Mensch in Religion, Philosophie und Naturwissenschaften* (Mainz, 1984), pp. 39-43.

(see, for example, the military colony Elephantine west of Aswan) and beyond that in large parts of the eastern Mediterranean region, there arose Jewish communities which, after the conquests of Alexander the Great, lay in the Hellenistic sphere of influence. Here the Jews made use of the colloquial Greek language, created the Greek translation of the Holy Scriptures, the „Septuagint," and many also acquired elements of a Greek literary and philosophical education.

2.2.3 Binitarian and Trinitarian Conceptions

In this environment the earliest triadic conceptions can be detected within the biblical religions and, indeed, in *three different series of motifs: in the tradition of wisdom, in angelology, and in the doctrine of the Logos.*
(1) From the middle of the 3rd century B.C. on, wisdom is increasingly hypostatized and gains a certain independence vis-à-vis God. Although it originates entirely from God – as creature „in the beginning" (Proverbs 8.22-3, the Wisdom of Jesus the Son of Sirach 24.9), as emerging „from the mouth of the Highest" (the Wisdom of Jesus the Son of Sirach 24.3), as „breath of God's power and pure effluent of the majesty of the Almighty" (Wisdom 7.25) – as „mediatrix Dei"[49] it takes over two important „divine" functions: (1) It functions as a demiurge taking part in the Creation and acts (2) in the history of the salvation of Israel or of mankind (Proverbs 8.22-31; the Wisdom of Jesus the Son of Sirach 24.1-22; Wisdom 7.22-27; 9.2); in the two more recent books – the Wisdom of Jesus the Son of Sirach, middle of the 2nd century B.C., and Wisdom, middle of the 1st century B.C. – wisdom has already come to be seen as the immanent principle of the cosmos constituting it deep down, and, in the book of Wisdom, even in the manner of an „unmoved mover" (7.24-27).
(2) The Old Testament already has angels very early on; they become theologically important from the Elohistic stratum of source texts in the Pentateuch as a result of their function of meditating between the transcendent Yahweh and Israel or history (cf. *maleách = angelos =* „messenger"). In early Judaism the transcendence of Yahweh is very strongly emphasized – and thus angels become more and more important. Conceptions from the religious milieu of Israel are also applied to them; often they are assigned to the divine sphere itself, are called „sons of God" or „spirits," and can be described as divine. Some angels receive names, above all Michael, the guardian angel of Israel, Gabriel, Raphael and Uriel.[50]

---

[49] G. Schimanowski, op. cit., p. 37.
[50] Cf. Georg Kretschmar, *Studien zur frühchristlichen Trinitätstheologie* (*Beiträge Historische Theologie*; Vol. 21), (Tübingen, 1956); Joseph Barbel, „Zur ‚Engel-Trinitätslehre' im Urchristentum," in *Theol. Revue* 54, 1958, pp. 49-58; Jean Daniélou, „Trinité et Angelologie

As a result in certain circles of early Judaism the attention of the devout was seldom directed at God alone, but at God *and* his court.[51] Among the angels, two of them – occasionally they are called Michael and Gabriel (e.g. the Second [Slavic] Book of Enoch 21.5; 22.8-10) – are soon able more and more to gain a special significance: they sit to the right and to the left of God and act outwardly on his behalf; in the rabbinical tradition they are described as „two divine standards" for the Creation. „In the concrete, graphic terms of the tradition these become the two hands of the Creator, with which He brings about the work of creation."[52]

The two angels are „two great and terrible mysteries before the eyes of God" (the Apocalypse of Moses 34; 1st century A.D.)[53]; they are the „glorious ones" who never leave the side of God by day or by night and stand „before the Lord ready to execute His commands" (Second [Slavic] Book of Enoch 21.1; before 70 A.D.).[54] *Philo* of Alexandria († 45-50 A.D.) philosophically deepened angelology and sees the „Father of the universe" – he refers to the epiphany of the three men before Abraham (Gen. 18) – as the Being in the middle, „on both sides, however, are the highest and nearest powers of the Being, the creative and the ruling powers; the creative power is called ‚God,' since with this power He posited the universe (into existence) and organized it, the ruling power, the ‚Lord,' since it is just that the Creator is lord over the Creation and rules it."[55] *Philo* also accepts the coexistence of „one" and „three" and tries – at least verbally – to reconcile them: „The fact, however, that the threefold representation refers in reality to a single object results not only from allegorical study, but also from the wording of the passage in the text."[56]

---

dans la théologie judéo-chrétienne," in *Resources de sciences religieuses* 45, 1957, pp. 5-41; Klaus Koch, „Monotheismus und Angelologie," in *Ein Gott allein?* loc. cit., pp. 565-581.

[51] Cf. Klaus Koch, „Monotheismus und Angelologie," loc. cit., p. 574: „At the outset the question was raised as to whether the success of monotheism is connected with the development of an angelology. ... A connection appears ... quite possible. Among the later Israelites leading circles are convinced of the pure and simple superiority of their god. Yet they do not believe in a distant, gray, bleak, abstract transcendence, but in a foundation of all reality that encounters mankind in manifest ways, so manifest that they can only be comprehended in the human mind to a limited extent."

[52] Leo Scheffczyk, „Lehramtliche Formulierungen und Dogmengeschichte der Trinität," in *Mysterium Salutis,* eds. J. Feiner and M. Löhrer, Vol. 2 (Einsiedeln, Zürich, Cologne, ^{1}1967), p. 155.

[53] German translation from Paul Riessler, *Altjüdisches Schrifttum außerhalb der Bibel* (Heidelberg, ^{2}1966), p. 151.

[54] German translation from P. Riessler, ibid., p. 459.

[55] „Über Abraham," p. 121, in *Philo von Alexandria: Die Werke in deutscher Übersetzung,* Vol. I, eds. L. Cohn, I. Heinemann, M. Adler, W. Theiler, et. al. (Berlin, ^{2}1962), pp. 121-122; cf. „Leben Moses," Vol. II, pp. 97-99.

[56] „Über Abraham," p. 131; German from *Philo von Alexandria: Die Werke in deutscher Übersetzung,* Vol. I, loc. cit., p. 124; cf. „Über die Cherubim," I.27-28, ibid. Vol. III (Berlin, ^{2}1962), p. 179.

(3) The concept of the Logos appears for the first time in *Heraclitus* in the sense of an unchanging cosmic law according to which all change and all variation occur. From *Plato* and *Aristotle* came new impulses by means of which the concept was used in a great variety of meanings in Hellenistic philosophy. Among the Stoics the Logos then turns into the symbol for the immanent cosmic „godhead." The Logos is also occasionally spoken of in early Judaism; it is usually then equated with „wisdom"[57] and identifies the demiurgical force with the help of which their god creates the cosmos and mankind: „God the Father and Lord of Compassion, thou who hast created the universe through thy *word* and who hast formed mankind through thy *wisdom* ..." (Wisdom 9.1-2).

Thus it was quite reasonable that *Philo* of Alexandria would also use the concept of the Logos in order „first of all to bridge the diastasis of God and world" and take advantage of it as a „mediator of Creation."[58]

In *Philo*'s speculation on the Logos, the third hypostasis is unimportant; in the foreground stand *God and his Logos*: „This most universal entity is God, and after him comes the divine Reason."[59] The one is „the divine Logos, the other however is the God placed over the Logos"; the latter is removed from all human knowledge, and „God Himself considers it below his dignity to come to sensuousness and sends his Logoi to help those who love virtue." In sensuousness one therefore encounters „not God any longer, but God Logos."[60] The Word is „mediator of all donation ..., by means of which He also created the world."[61] The Word is the first „work" of God,[62] but preceding all other things.[63]

What, then, has happened to the idea of God in early Judaism? Quite obviously under the influence of Hellenistic thinking Yahweh came to be attributed a transcendence in the Greek sense, which associated Him with immutability of being, non-acting, simplicity. That, however, meant that He could not, as would have been the case in accordance with Jewish tradition, Himself function any longer as the creator of the world and lord or ruler of the history of Israel and the tribes. For the exercising of both of these functions insolubly linked with Yahweh, lesser divine mediatory figures dependent upon Yahweh were required. In other words: the economic activities of God, the demiurgical and

---

[57] Cf. Wisdom 9.1-2; 18.14-16; Slavic Enoch 33.9.

[58] R. Schnackenburg, „Logos," in *LThK*² 6, p. 1124.

[59] „Allegorische Erklärung des heiligen Gesetzbuches II," 86; in Philo von Alexandrien, *Die Werke in deutscher Übersetzung*, Vol. III, op. cit., p. 79.

[60] „Über die Träume I," 61-70; German translation from Philo von Alexandrien, eds. L. Cohn et al., Vol. VI (Berlin, ²1962), pp. 185-188.

[61] „Über die Unveränderlichkeit Gottes," 57; German translation from Philo von Alexandrien, eds. L. Cohn et al., Vol IV (Berlin, ²1962), p. 85.

[62] „Über die Opfer Abels und Kains," 65; German translation from Philo von Alexandrien, Vol. III, op. cit., p. 241.

[63] Ibid., p. 66.

those relating to salvation history, were separated in early Judaism – as a necessary consequence of Hellenization – from the completely *unchangeable* and *one* God, hence from a god that was to be kept away from change and plurality, and were turned into (lesser) divine hypostases, whereby this could take place either in a mythical-narrative (angelology) or mythical-„philosophical" way (wisdom tradition, doctrine of the Logos); the hypostatization could also effect each of the two functions for itself – then there were *two* angels, which led to a divine *triad* – or could be anchored in a single hypostasis – then just *one* wisdom or *one* Logos was sufficient, a *binitarian conception*; in the latter case a functional doubling *within* the second hypostasis can be identified: wisdom or Logos function demiurgically *and* with regard to salvation history.

The hypostatization of the functions of god made it possible for the Diaspora Jews to add to the *God of their Fathers, Yahweh*, hence to the historically acting God, the *god of the Greeks*, a world-immanent principle, which in the meantime they likewise „needed." Belonging as they did to both cultural areas and apparently having had internalized their respective understandings of existence, it seems that the religious answer of *one* tradition was no longer sufficient for them. As Jews they continued to place all their hopes in Yahweh, who founded history, directs it and conducts it to its end; *but as Greeks they also needed the god who constitutes the world not only from the outside, but from the inside, from the middle of its being.* Increasingly they introduced ideas of this kind into the concept of wisdom, but above all they had recourse to the Logos, the impersonal, immanent principle of this cosmos.

The use of the concept of the Logos here is not to be viewed as a specific theological achievement of *Philo*; the *prologue to the Gospel according to St. John*, originally a pre-Christian hymn that was prayed in the services of Jewish-Hellenistic congregations shows that the idea of a Logos as an immanent demiurgical principle next to God was widespread. „In the beginning was the Word, and the Word was with God, and the Logos was God (divine). The same was in the beginning with God. All things were made by him; and without him was not any thing made that was made ..." (John 1.1-3).

That the desire to introduce the Greek conception of god is also playing a role here is likewise visible in the fact that connected with the Logos was in particular its *demiurgical* function. That is also why it „is" (only) „in the beginning" (Gen. 1.1); together with the formation of the world, the hypostatization of its ground was required. The activity relating to the history of salvation, which was more important for the Jewish religion, was foreign in terms of this conceptual framework of its genesis and was only added to it secondarily – in the prologue to the Gospel according to St. John through its Christological additions. Probably the Hellenistic dominance in conceptual history is the reason why, in these cases, although the historical activity of God is recorded, it is not decisive, and thus is, unlike in the more „Jewish" angelology, *not* the result *of its own hypostasis* into an – in addition to the demiurgy – independent hypostasis.

The conflict between unity and plurality in God was at the time, due to the absolute dominance of Yahweh, of God as such, and to the resulting subordination of the second or of the second and third hypostases („subordinationism"), not yet so radically felt. Certainly, the Hellenistic milieu, in which plural structurings of God, polytheism, were a matter of course, contributed to this. The doctrine *of the double nature of the Logos*, which on the one hand is eternally in God and identical with Him (as *lógos endiáthetos*, as the God of the immanent Logos), but which on the other hand had emerged for the purpose of the creation of the world „in the beginning" out of God (*lógos proforikós*) and then became in this „independent," hypostatized form the principle of the Creation, represents a conscious effort to convey unity with duality in a theoretical way as well. The schema is tangible in *Philo*, in the pre-Christian part of the *prologue to the Gospel according to St. John* and in the early Christian *apologists*. Heady with the beautiful concepts, the general public only much later became aware, although it had theoretically already been pointed out by *Origen*, that the Logos emerging „in the beginning" had to be thought of as temporal, changeable and creaturely, so that it is in any case a different logos than the Logos immanent to God, with which it has in common only the word Logos, and not what is meant by it: The *one* Logos is only another name for God; the *second* Logos is a separate divine entity originated from „God as such" with a temporal beginning.

2.3 The End and a New Beginning

The development of the thinking about God described above soon came to an end in Judaism. The defeats in the wars against Rome in the first and second century and the loss of many of the factors that until then had formed its identity – the Temple, Jerusalem, etc. – forced a reorientation which was then sought in a closer contact with the Palestinian tradition and in a limiting of the many Hellenistic influences. The cultural „re-Palestinization" ended the previous binitarian and Trinitarian development and reestablished a monotheism unmodified by plurality.

To the extent that Christianity arose in Palestine, it is in turn in its origins closer to the roots of the Jewish religion; the preaching of Jesus and the Palestinian Christianity which was close to it provide no point of departure for a doctrine of the Trinity. Scarcely arisen, however, the new movement passed itself on into the Hellenistic world of the Roman Empire; the inherited monotheism was once more confronted with Greek ideas and the motifs that had already been active in early Judaism came to life again. When after several generations the ethnic Jewish groups became a minority in the Christian communities and „heathen Christians" began to determine the theology, many of the previous inhibitions with regard to the numbers two and three in God disappeared. However, in one large old church, the Syrian, the desire for a God who was (also) cosmic was not able to gain a foothold; here a pure monotheism lived on for a long time.

3. Trinitarian Echoes in the New Testament?

One can probably assume that a Christian doctrine of the Trinity would have never come into being if there had not been the order to baptize (Matt. 28.19) or the account of the baptism of Jesus (Mark 1.9-11). This, however is true solely for the mechanisms of formal legitimation, not for the actual causalities. The latter must be sought *outside of the contexts of the New Testament* and are, as far as they are concerned, the reason for interpreting New Testament motifs, including those mentioned, in a Trinitarian sense – against their intentions; since this collection of writings contains no Trinitarian propositions, and only in a few texts can the hesitant beginnings of a binitarian development be identified.

3.1 Jesus and God

There is no indication that Jesus would have understood the „father," from whom he felt himself to have been sent and to whom he probably felt himself to be related in a special way, differently than the monotheistic God of Judaism; the triadic conceptions of early Judaism seem not to have been known to him. This consensus of New Testament research need not be more closely examined here.

Nevertheless, there are attempts to see even the later doctrine of the Trinity in relation to Jesus. *Franz Josef Schierse* writes: „If the belief in the Trinity is not to be a speculation in a vacuum, it must stand in some kind of connection with the experience of belief of Jesus."[64] For this reason *Schierse* with many other exegetes and an even greater number of systematists are trying to demonstrate connections between Jesus and Trinitarian conceptions.

That, however, is difficult unless one practices eisegesis. Naturally, if one absolutely wants to, one can make plausible certain triadic structures in the Word of Jesus, as in *any* religious experience if, for instance, God appears as beginning and end of history, if Jesus attributes himself a certain (even present) relevance and also knows the perspective on the future succession. Here, however, it is a question of aspects which result as a matter of course out of the temporal dimension of human experiences, but without their being able to be simply consolidated in a Trinitarian fashion.

It is historically correct that God was called Father by Jesus and for this reason he could quite well have understood himself as „son" in a special sense – an explicit Word of Jesus is lacking. However, the constantly repeated recourse to a filial relationship, which could then later be rightly interpreted in a binitarian sense, is simply false because it finds no support in the texts and contradicts

---

[64] F.J. Schierse, „Die neutestamentlich Trinitätsoffenbarung," in *Mysterium Salutis*, Vol. II, op. cit., p. 94.

everything we know about Jesus. At the least the filial relationship in the understanding of Jesus did not go beyond that which in the tradition for all of Israel was characterized as „son," or was claimed for its king: in the history of salvation Jesus represents God like a son; he thus saw himself as close to God in a special way. However, it is historically refutable that at that time it „was quite unusual to address God simply with ‚Abba'"[65] or as „Father." This kind of form of address was common in early Judaism,[66] and nobody would have had the idea of attributing a divine being to those who used it. Thus the form of addressing the father used by Jesus reveals a good deal about the significance he lays claim to in terms of the history of salvation, but it is in no way an indication of binitarian conceptions. Just as little should the Spirit, in the event Jesus himself spoke of the Spirit at all (perhaps only in Mark 3.28-30; the sins „against the Holy Ghost"), be interpreted as a proper hypostasis.

Hence the question arises whether, in reversing the above-cited statements by *Schierse*, one would have to summarize by concluding as follows: Are the Trinitarian conceptions to be considered as speculations since they demonstrably have no recognizable connection with the preaching of Jesus?

3.2 The New Testament Tradition after Jesus

3.2.1 The Palestinian-Christian and the Diaspora Jewish-Christian Tradition

All of the writings of the New Testament were composed by Diaspora Jewish Christians – probably even Luke should be counted among them. This was a stroke of luck for the later assimilation of Christianity in the Roman Empire, since these writings formed a bridge from its „foreign" Palestinian beginnings to its new addressee, Hellenistic culture.

To the extent that the ideas of the Palestinian groups of Jewish Christians still close to Jesus, among whom his disciples should be counted, can be recognized in the New Testament, they resemble those of Jesus in our question: God is the monotheistic Yahweh of Israel; there is no indication of binitarian or Trinitarian thinking.

Soon, however, Greek language and interpretational frameworks were able to spread in the communities. Yet, nevertheless, there were still no identifiable upheavals in the thinking about god; almost all of the texts of the New Testament are entirely shaped by Jewish monotheism, which however – and without itself having been corrected – is already combined with characteristics

---

[65] As in F.J. Schierse, ibid., p. 93.
[66] Cf. Angelika Strotmann, *Mein Vater bist du (Sir. 51.10). Zur Bedeutung der Vaterschaft Gottes in kanonischen und nichtkanonischen frühjüdischen Schriften*, Frankfurter Theologische Studien, Vol. 39 (Frankfurt, 1991).

that are borrowed from the Greek tradition: God appears increasingly as omnipotent, omniscient, unchanging, as the supreme being, etc.

In Christology Jesus is indeed already given sovereign titles such as „*kyrios*" (= lord), in the Greek translation of the Old Testament a title of Yahweh's, and the „Son of God," whereby he would certainly be shifted into the proximity of God, nevertheless these symbolic terms are in no way understood in the sense of a „quality" relating to the being of Jesus, but as descriptions of his role in the history of salvation: Just like Israel or even its kings, Jesus is the „Son of God," i.e., he represents Him through his historical action. The spirit (of God) does not play any appreciable role in the Palestinian-Christian strata of the tradition; only in the later texts formed by Diaspora Jewish Christians does Jesus act – though seldom – full of spirit, but without the spirit being anything more than a *dynamis* or power of God Himself.

The theologians of the Synoptic Gospels, who after all represent a main current in the history of Christian theology up to the nineties of the first century, do not in any way recognize divinity in terms of the being of Jesus and thus recognize neither a necessity for a binitarian structuring of God nor a divine spirit which they would need to distinguish from „God as such." *Joachim Gnilka*, for example, describes in an excursus on the „virgin birth" a broad consensus in Biblical studies: „Jesus' human being out of the Spirit and the Virgin, as it is known in the prehistory of Mark and Luke, still does not presuppose his preexistence and becoming human. Both are at least not obvious in the Synoptic Gospels. The Christological development went in this direction in the (ante-)Pauline and (ante-)Johannine domain. ... Only later were both stages of development united."[67]

Thus it is also already possible to establish something fundamental concerning the interpretation of the order to baptize in Matthew and concerning the account of the baptism of Jesus in texts of the Synoptic authors: They too cannot be understood in terms of a concept of the Trinity.

The success of the Christian mission had a good deal to do with the straightforwardness of its preaching: „In the process, above all the mission borne among the heathens by Christians of Jewish descent profited from the attractiveness of Biblical Jewish monotheism. ... The well-known uniqueness of God in the ‚Sch^{e}ma Israel' was without question the precondition of the Christian mission"[68] whose „message" was reflected in the New Testament.

---

[67] Joachim Gnilka, „Das Matthäusevangelium, 1. Teil: Kommentar zu Kap. 1,1-13,58" in *Herders Theologischer Kommentar zum Neuen Testament* (Freiburg, Basel, Wien, 1986), p. 31.

[68] Michael Theobald, „Gott, Logos und Pneuma. ‚Trinitarische' Rede von Gott im Johannesevangelium," in *Monotheismus und Christologie*, ed. Hans-Josef Klauck (*Quaestiones Disputatae*, Vol. 138) (Freiburg, Basel, Wien, 1992), p. 42.

3.2.2 Beginnings of a Hellenistic Christology[69]

Only in one regard can one speak of – an indeed not Trinitarian, but at least – a binitarian tendency in the New Testament: In pieces of text in which Hellenistic thinking begins to determine the Christological reception, one can identify the orientation towards the assertion of a divinity of Jesus in terms of his being; as it was expressed in the previous quote from *Gnilka*, echoes of this kind can be found in the Pauline and Johannine writings, as well as in the traditions employed by them. Admittedly, in them, for instance in the ante-Pauline hymn to the Philippians (Phil. 2.6-11) or in the ante-Johannine parts of the prologue to the Gospel according to St. John (John 1.1-14), Jewish-historical thinking still sets the tone, to the extent that, for example, in the hymn to the Philippians the raising of Jesus to God is a consequence of his obedience to the cross and not simply the natural assertion of the right given to him by his divine being. Nevertheless, in this passage, which is in no way free of tension, Jesus *also* appears as one descended from the divine sphere, in the prologue to the Gospel according to St. John even as the incarnated Logos. He is given divine being and thus a pre-birth existence.

This incarnation Christology (Jesus is God incarnated) is in the New Testament thus still combined with an elevation Christology (Jesus is raised to the divine dignity on the basis of his historical action), and that, even though the two are in point of fact mutually contradictory and incompatible with each other: In the one case, Christ is already eternally God, in the other he is only raised to this dignity after his death, naturally without then *being* the real God – one cannot *become* God. The two Christologies are arranged all the way through one beside the other without being conciliated with one another.

This inconsistency shows how novel and foreign the Hellenistic incarnation Christology, or a Christology which tends to give Jesus a second, divine nature, was at first felt to be; one probably considered it indispensable that it was then combined with the older elevation ideas. All the same, however, a new Christological understanding, which was also to have consequences for the conception of God, is announcing itself in these texts: If Jesus in a preexistent form always already belonged to the divine sphere, then he would have to receive a place in God next to the Father, and thus be intellectually different from him. God becomes doubly structured: There is God as such, the Father, but Jesus is also „God" – whereby, for example, in the Pauline Epistles or in the prologue to the Gospel according to St. John the former is „*ho theós*," *the* God, but Jesus is „*theós*" (without the definite article) in the predicative sense of „divine."

Only in places in the New Testament where one can find this kind of Christology, which was indispensable for the Hellenistic soteriological reception of Jesus and which was able to predominate in the following centuries, can one speak of echoes of a binitarian development; but since the

---

[69] On what follows cf. by the present author, *Fundamentalchristologie*, loc. cit., pp. 98-132.

Spirit was not sifted out as its own hypostasis within the divine sphere, there was no Biblical support for an even more far-reaching Trinitarian structure.

3.2.3 Triadic Formulas in the New Testament

Although the New Testament does not contain Trinitarian concepts, in some passages it nevertheless contains triadic combinations of the Father, Son or Jesus, and Spirit; in theological history after the New Testament as soon as the course was set in favor of a Trinitarian development, these passages were then seen and used – and, despite better exegetical judgment, are often still used – as Biblical evidence for a new conception of God.
In the authentic *Pauline Epistles* there are three passages, one of which (Gal. 4.4-7)[70] summarizes the Christian faith in condensed form, the other two (1 Cor. 12.1-8; 2 Cor. 13.14) serve rhetorically to reinforce a train of thought (the thought of unity in 1 Cor. 12.4-8)[71] or a salutation (2 Cor. 13.14)[72]; triadic formulas of this kind were at the time a popular rhetorical device, as, for instance, 1 John 5.8 can demonstrate: „For there are three that bear witness in earth, the spirit, and the water, and the blood: and these three agree in one."
Although the Pauline passages show that, on the one hand, the naming of the one God, Jesus Christ and the (Holy) Spirit are part of the core of the message and that, on the other hand, the Spirit of God belonging to the Jewish tradition is now at the same time the Spirit of Jesus which calls „Abba, Father" (Gal. 4.6) in us, none of the cited passages – to the least extent – gives rise to a Trinitarian understanding of God; even the filiation or the lordship of Jesus, as well as the function of the Spirit, are described in terms of the history of salvation and are not even distantly considered to be being-like intradivine hypostases.

---

[70] Gal. 4.4-7: „ ⁴But when the fullness of the time was come, God sent forth his Son, made of a woman, made under the law, ⁵To redeem them that were under the law, that we might receive the adoption of sons. ⁶And because ye are sons, God hath sent forth the Spirit of his Son into your hearts, crying, Abba, Father. ⁷Wherefore thou art no more a servant, but a son; and if a son, then an heir of God through Christ."

[71] 1 Cor. 12.1-8: „ ¹Now concerning spiritual gifts, brethren, I would not have you ignorant. ²Ye know that ye were Gentiles, carried away to these dumb idols, even as ye were led. ³Wherefore I give you to understand that no man speaking by the Spirit of God called Jesus accursed: and that no man can say that Jesus is the Lord, but by the Holy Ghost. ⁴Now there are diversities of gifts, but the same Spirit. ⁵And there are differences of administrations, but the same Lord. ⁶And there are diversities of operations, but it is the same God which worketh all in all. ⁷But the manifestation of the Spirit is given to every man to profit withal. ⁸For to one is given by the Spirit the word of wisdom; to another the world of knowledge by the same Spirit. ...."

[72] 2 Cor. 13.14: „The grace of the Lord Jesus Christ, and the love of God, and the communion of the Holy Ghost, be with you all. Amen."

For this reason it is understandable that these „trinities" are not taken up, much less deepened, by the *Deuteropaulines* which were written much, much later. They pass on only a single triadic passage in which, however, the third position is not taken by the Spirit, but – as in the early Jewish tradition – by angels (1 Tim. 5.21): „I charge thee before God, and the Lord Jesus Christ, and the elect angels. ..."

In a sense similar to that in Gal. 4.4-7, Peter's speech in the version found in the Acts of the Apostles (2.32-36)[73] provides a brief summary of the essentials of the Christian faith in three steps, whereby the Christology is quite clearly an elevation Christology and the Spirit appears as a force of God Himself – hence here too there is no triadic understanding of God. Much the same can also be said of the salutation in the *1st Epistle of St. Peter* (1.2).[74]

Thus there yet remain the two most important passages in terms of historical impact, the order to baptize at the end of the Gospel according to St. Matthew and the Synoptic account of the baptism of Jesus in the Jordan. Previously, it has already been indicated that the Synoptic tradition has neither the idea of a being-like divinity of Jesus, nor a proper Spirit hypostasis, and therefore provides no hint of Trinitarian ideas.

Yet how is the order to baptize in Matt. 28.19 to be understood then? It reads: „Go ye therefore, and teach all nations, baptizing them in the name of the Father, and of the Son, and of the Holy Ghost. ..." This triadic lineup is conspicuous because in other New Testament references to baptism mention is only made of a baptism „in the name of Jesus Christ" (Acts 2.38; 10.48) or „in the name of the Lord Jesus" (Acts 8.16; 19.5; cf. 1 Cor. 1.13,15). The baptism formula had thus been „triadically" modified in the meantime, by the time of the Gospel according to St. Matthew.

The transition, however, from baptism in the name of Jesus to a triadic formula is thoroughly explainable: As long as the young Christianity was taking its mission predominately to Jewish fellow believers in Palestine and in the Diaspora, the documentation of the conversion of a Jew to Christianity was *linguistically sufficient* if he had himself baptized „in the name of Jesus." Yet when „heathens" wished to join up with Christianity, this formula was *no longer adequate*; they had to abandon the polytheism they had inherited and profess their faith in the *one Father*; the conversion to Christianity included the

---

[73] Acts 2.32-36: „ [32]This Jesus hath God raised up, whereof we all are witnesses. [33]Therefore being by the right hand of God exalted, and having received of the Father the promise of the Holy Ghost, he hath shed forth this, which ye now see and hear. [34]For David is not ascended into the heavens: but he saith himself, The LORD said unto my Lord, Sit thou on my right hand, [35]Until I make thy foes thy footstool. [36]Therefore let all the house of Israel know assuredly, that God hath made that same Jesus, whom ye have crucified, both Lord and Christ."

[74] 1 Pt. 1.2: „... Elect according to the foreknowledge of God and Father, through sanctification of the Spirit, unto obedience and sprinkling of the blood of Jesus Christ: Grace unto you, and peace, be multiplied."

recognition of Jesus, the Son; likewise, they could no longer continue to live their lives according to their former practices and had to follow Jesus, and hence live their lives according to his *Spirit*. In other words: The baptism formula at the end of the Gospel according to St. Matthew reflects the situation of the heathen mission and briefly summarizes the three central changes that were characteristic of the conversion to Christianity in this milieu and whose communication also probably represented the essential objective of the baptismal catechesis: „The Trinitarian baptismal formula can thus be quite easily comprehended as a summary of the baptismal catechesis."[75]

Something similar is also true for the sole narrative passage in which the Father, Son and Spirit appear, *the baptism of Jesus* in Mark 1.9-11: „[9]And it came to pass in those days, that Jesus came from Nazareth of Galilee, and was baptized of John in Jordan. [10]And straightway coming up out of the water, he saw the heavens opened, and the Spirit like a dove descending upon him: [11]And there came a voice from heaven, saying, *Thou art my beloved Son, in whom I am well pleased.*"

The baptism of Jesus by John is certainly to be taken as a historical fact, precisely because the tradition that Jesus was a disciple or pupil of the Baptist does not at all fit into the later Christology; and thus the Gospels depict the relationship – the more recent a stratum is, the more clearly – between the Baptist and Jesus in a reversed sense: he is a precursor, not worthy of untying his shoes, etc. (Only the words of Jesus concerning the Baptist as the greatest of men [Matt. 11.11] still let one imagine the original circumstances.)

The baptism of Jesus has in the Gospel according to St. Mark in the above-mentioned Christological tendency been simultaneously handed down with a theological correction and a profession of faith: The voice from heaven and the Spirit enthrone Jesus with the adoption formula (v. 11b) as the Messiah (whereby the stage of a baptism by John the Baptist is far exceeded) and at the same time summarize in narrative form what is at stake in the later *Christian* baptism: the acceptance of each baptized person by God[76] and his Spirit, which has been anticipated by means of an example in Jesus.

More than this should not be read into the baptism story: „God is One. The monotheistic profession of faith is firmly anchored in the Gospel according to St. Mark,"[77] and much the same is also true for the Gospels according to St. Matthew[78] and St. Luke.[79] „Thus the idea of God in the Jesus tradition proves, in the aspects we have observed, to be one characterized by the Biblical-Jewish

---

[75] F.-J. Schierse, loc. cit., p. 126.

[76] Cf. F.-J. Schierse, loc. cit., p. 100: „... at stake is a piece of baptismal catechesis intended to teach the theological significance of the Christian sacrament. the believer is accepted by God in the baptism and is endowed with the Holy Spirit of filiation."

[77] Joachim Gnilka, „Zum Gottesgedanken in der Jesusüberlieferung" in *Monotheismus und Christologie*, loc. cit., p. 151.

[78] Cf. the same, ibid., p. 157.

[79] Cf. the same, ibid., pp. 159-162.

image of God."⁸⁰ Even the Gospel according to St. John has no triadic formulas, „but a few texts with a corresponding structure. ... For, just as one cannot talk in a Johannine sense of God without speaking of his Son, Jesus of Nazareth (cf.1.18), so also not without speaking of the Spirit of God. ..."⁸¹ In statements such as these, however, there is the danger of reading the texts on the basis of a later development; even the Gospel according to St. John gives no Trinitarian indications.

In sum: Triadic arrangements can be found, it is true, only relatively infrequently, in the New Testament. They are in no way indications of a Trinitarian differentiation in God himself; rather they summarize the three core elements of the Christian faith – the *one* God, Jesus Christ, a life from the Spirit – in condensed form or in the sense of rhetorical reinforcement. They were, however, taken up in the later development and understood as Biblical references as soon as Trinitarian thinking began to evolve.

Now it is thoroughly understandable that again and again in theology New Testament starting points are sought for triadic speech or even for an immanent doctrine of the Trinity. In the opinion of *Hans Urs von Balthasar*: „However, there is no other entrance to the Trinitarian mystery than its revelation in Jesus Christ and in the Holy Spirit, and no statement on the immanent Trinity ought to distance itself even one foot from the basis of the New Testament. ..."⁸² Normative theses of this kind are, however, only possible if the New Testament is not read historically-critically, that is – even approximately – in the way it was meant to be read.

In the meantime, though, it has been more clearly realized by many, even by systematic theologians, that „with the help of an exegesis of individual New Testament texts"⁸³ one does not get anywhere in the attempt to establish the doctrine of the Trinity Biblically. Yet to avoid abandoning such substantiation, one looks for ways out of the dilemma. *Gisbert Greshake* thus writes: „One should, however, make a point of stressing the New Testament ‚basic experience': At the center of the original Christian experience stands the insight that Jesus of Nazareth out of his own authority and competence gives man God, that – in other words – through him as the Son and in the Holy Spirit, God the Father has gone to mankind and has 'communicated' himself totally to it."⁸⁴

It will remain to be seen whether the Christian „original experience" has been accurately described here and whether in a collection of texts like the New Testament one can disregard the „individual texts" – which is what it consists of, after all. Yet even if there was an original experience such as this, how can an *immanent* Trinity be justified with it? *Greshake* has even suggested a

---

⁸⁰ The same, ibid., p. 162.
⁸¹ M. Theobald, loc. cit., p. 64.
⁸² *Theologik*, Vol. II (Einsiedeln, ²1985), p. 117.
⁸³ G. Greshake, *Der dreieine Gott*, loc. cit., p. 48.
⁸⁴ Ibid., pp. 48, 49.

solution for this: „Jesus Christ and the Holy Spirit are not ‚mediums' separate from God, through which God would act, while himself remaining withdrawn in the background as a concealed, inaccessible abyss; rather the ‚mediation forms,' in which God reaches out to people, are themselves *God*. ... Now if the ‚mediums' of this self-giving of God are divine, then God himself must be characterized by internal differentiations. ..." For this reason He is „Trinity ‚giving communication' in itself."[85] Of course, with an exegesis of this sort anything can be backed up Biblically, even the immanent Trinity. However, if one keeps to the texts – as well as to an experience on which they are based – one must do without verbalisms of this kind.

---

[85] Ibid., pp. 49, 50.

4. The Origins of a Christian Doctrine of the Binity or the Trinity between the 2nd Century and the Beginning of the 4th Century

4.1 The Theological-Historical Situation

4.1.1 Two New Areas of Activity for God

The Christian doctrine of the Trinity, in its oldest version, first originated in the era after the New Testament, in the second and early third century. What typifies it is that, as already before in Hellenized early Judaism, it *sorts out God's two largest „externally-directed" areas of activity*, the creation of the world (demiurgy) and his salvation activity in history (economy in the narrower sense; more broadly conceived, the Creation is also included in the term), *as separate divine hypostases.*

However, the „new religion," Christianity, brought in *two further areas of God's activity*, or better, historical concretions resulting from the specific difference from the Jewish mother religion. Already in the Jewish religion the action of God in history can be seen in exemplary fashion from his power over Israel; in Christianity, in addition to that, further „specifications" become important: (above all) the action of God *in Jesus* and (also) *in the Church*. The Greek interpretation of this economic action of God in Israel (preparatory) and in Jesus (final), as well as – through his Spirit – in the Church, must have promoted the tendencies to their hypostatization. Above all, Christology and then also „ecclesiology" gave the economic doctrine of the binity and the Trinity a strong push or made them inevitable in terms of the history of theology: The salvation function of Jesus is hypostatized into the divine sphere or, conversely, in Jesus a divine hypostasis has appeared. Here the Incarnation was from the beginning closely connected with the demiurgical activity, so that already in the few passages of the New Testament that are more strongly Hellenistic Jesus was in his preexistent way of being also the principle of the Creation (cf. the prologue to the Gospel of St. John or Col. 1.16,17).

For an even longer period of time uncertainty existed concerning the establishment – in addition to God and the Logos – of a third hypostasis. Just as in early Judaism demiurgical and salvation-historical functions were often a matter of one hypostasis (then there was – the binitarian – „God and Wisdom" or „God and his Logos"), so also in early Christianity. Often it is therefore the Logos itself which has spoken through the Father, which has been incarnated in Jesus (cf. the Epistle to the Hebrews) *and* which, as present and working Christ or his Spirit (with no recognizable hypostatic differentiation), sanctifies his disciples; then it sufficed to think God along binitarian lines, and this is also what took place again and again until the fourth century when the Spirit was finally sanctioned as a hypostasis of its own. Occasionally, however, there can be found – although scarcely emphasized – a hypostatization of the economic-ecclesiological function specifically in the Holy Spirit; then *the Spirit* came to be viewed as the one who had already spoken through the fathers, brought about the Incarnation of the Logos and was now leading and sanctifying the Church. In addition to the hypostasis of the Logos, that of the Spirit, which had to be distinguished from it, became necessary.

The reason for the origin of a Christian doctrine of the Trinity since the 2nd century are thus *on the one hand* identical with those that led to the development of triadic ideas in early Judaism: The syncretism of two cultural religions made it necessary to have both concepts of God side by side and to connect them with each other – the „historical-transcendent" God Yahweh or Father of Jesus and the „immanent-transcendent" God of the Hellenistic forms of religion. *One* variant alone did not suffice: The Hellenists placing themselves as Christians in the monotheistic tradition also still „needed" their deeply internalized cosmic principle. And as time passed, the more strongly the communities were characterized by Hellenistic majorities, the more the inhibitions regarding the number „two" (or „three") in God were dropped.

Beyond the early Judaic motifs, however, the doctrine of the Trinity also has a *specifically Christian root*, namely *Christology* and *ecclesiology*. Although in their oldest variations of a Jewish-Christian sort, in which Jesus – simplified – was considered as an eschatalogical human being, these would have in no way made a correction of monotheism necessary; the Hellenistic Christology already announcing itself in tentative beginnings in the New Testament, according to which Jesus is the incarnated preexistent Logos of God, made the sorting out from God of a second hypostasis nearly inevitable.

This is not true in the same way for the hypostatization of the Spirit; if one considers the course of the discussions from the 2nd to the 4th century, the Spirit finally seems to have been included more in accordance with one's duty, out of loyalty to the triadic formulas – meanwhile viewed as a series of divine hypostases – in the New Testament, and above all to the baptism formula.

4.1.2 The Most Significant Cultural Characteristics of the Early Christian Church

In the course of the 2nd century Christianity spread into the cities around the Mediterranean, at first usually taking as its starting points the synagogue communities. Here the *Jewish-Christian* members represented the core of the communities, but the non-Jewish Christians increased in number and thus also in the force of their influence upon the theology. *Palestinian Christianity* was considerably weakened by the armed conflicts between the Jews and the Roman state in the first (the destruction of Jerusalem in the year 70) and the second century (the Bar Kokba revolts around 135); many such Christians were forced to immigrate to Syria, were increasingly felt to be heretical by Hellenistic

Christians and around the middle of the 2nd century were expelled from the Church (disputes with the „Ebionites," who – in the sense of the Christological beginnings – viewed Jesus as a „mere human being"). For a while the *Diaspora Jewish-Christians* were still able to assert a greater influence, but they too became a minority from the 2nd half of the 2nd century on; from then onwards their theology was primarily still represented in a literary form by the New Testament and no longer by dynamic communities.

Hellenistic soteriological motifs, about which a word or two has already been said, subsequently exerted more and more of an influence on the thinking. Within the Hellenistic portions of the spreading Church, however, there were *two regional variations* in which individual ideas and conceptual frameworks played a role: Indeed, already very early on Christianity was widespread in *Syria*, whose western part, although Hellenized, nevertheless continued to cultivate the native Semitic way of thinking, and toward the end of the 2nd century, at first in North Africa, a *Latin theology* also begins timidly to establish itself.

The history of theology of the 2nd century is thus by no means uniform and can also not be represented in one way as if only *one* line of development were important. On the contrary, there were various communities, mentalities and theologies. In them the ideas about God are quite different, although – due to the dominance of Hellenistic thought in the area of the Empire – the Christian designs growing *out of that area*, precisely the Trinitarian ones, remained victorious.

4.2 The Central Variations in the Concept of God until around the End of the 2nd Century

4.2.1 Jewish-Christian Traditions

4.2.1.1 The Jewish Profession of Faith in the Monotheistic God

The literature which is united under the term „Apostolic Fathers" but which is very disparate in its genres, chronological origins and objectives, documents, except for the epistles of *Ignatius* of Antioch († 117) and the Second Epistle of St. Clement (before 150), a Jewish-Christian Christology: Jesus is the „servant of God" as it says in the *Martydom of St. Polycarp*[86] composed in the sixties or

---

[86] Martydom of St. Polycarp 14.1: „Lord, God, Almighty, Father of this beloved and promised servant, Jesus Christ ..., God of the angels and powers. ..." God is praised for participation in the martydom „for the resurrection of the eternal life ... in the immortality of the Holy Spirit" (eds. Andreas Lindemann, Henning Paulsen, *Die Apostolischen Väter: griechisch-deutsche Parallelausgabe* [Tübingen, 1992], p. 275).

seventies of the 2nd century and in the *Didache*[87] which, though written around 110-120, is often older in terms of its material. This Christological title refers back to the servant-of-God songs of the prophet in exile (6th C. B.C.), whose name is unknown to us and whose sayings are appended to the Book of Isaiah. Thus it is to be understood completely in terms of the Jewish-Christian history of salvation, although otherwise numerous Hellenistic motifs are clearly being picked up.[88] This means, however, that there is no reason at all to distinguish in God a second hypostasis, a divine way of being which would later be incarnated in Jesus. And thus the few triadic formulas,[89] as in the New Testament, are not to be understood as an indication of Trinitarian thinking.

Even the Christology of the *First Epistle of St. Clement*, a text addressed on behalf of the Roman parish to the parish in Corinth around 97, is more Jewish-Christian in its orientation: There is God, the Creator of the universe, and „his beloved servant, Jesus Christ, our Lord."[90] In another passage – again from the Jewish tradition – he is called the „high priest of our sacrificial offerings,"[91] but also – probably more Hellenistically – the mirror of the countenance of God and intermediary of the gnosis.[92] In any case nothing suggests the need to ascribe to him a preexistent hypostasis. Twice the epistle reports on triadic formulas,[93] but in no way whatsoever do they, as *J.A. Fischer* believes, form a „Trinity,"[94] rather they do not even go beyond that which the New Testament already provides.

---

[87] The text in *Didache* 10.2 is part of the oldest Eucharistic high prayer: „We thank thee, Holy Father, for thy holy name, which thou hast suffered to take up residence in our hearts, and for the knowledge and the faith and the immortality which thou hast proclaimed to us through Jesus, thy servant; (may) glory be thine forever" (eds. Lindemann/Paulsen, op. cit., p. 15).

[88] In the text of the *Didache*, for example, it is a question of gnosis and immortality; God is characterized as the Almighty, as omnipotent; the function of Jesus is the imparting of knowledge, etc.

[89] E.g. the Martyrdom of St. Polycarp 14.1 (see note 2) and 22.1: „We say to you, farewell, Brothers, who live in the word of Jesus Christ, which is in accordance with the Gospel: with it glory be to God the Father and the Holy Spirit ... " (ibid. Lindemann/Paulsen, loc. cit., p. 283); cf. *Didache* 1 (with a citation of the baptism formula according to St. Matthew).

[90] *1 Clem.* 59.2 (ed. Joseph A. Fischer, *Die Apostolischen Väter*, introd., ed., trans. and annotated by J.A. Fischer [München, Darmstadt, ¹1956], p. 13).

[91] 36.1 (ed. Fischer, op. cit., p. 71); cf. 48.4: „gateway of righteousness" (ed. Fischer, op. cit., p. 85); cf. 22.1.

[92] 36.2 (ibid.).

[93] 46.6: „Or do we not have a God and a Christ and a Spirit of mercy ...?" (ed. Fischer, op. cit., p. 83), and 58.1,2 (in particular 2: „... For there lives God and there lives the Lord Jesus Christ and the Holy Spirit" (ed. Fischer, op. cit., p. 99); cf. 42.3.

[94] Op. cit., p. 13.

4.2.1.2 The Survival of Early Jewish Angelology

The early Jewish angelology – probably at first in circles of Jewish Christianity and later outside of them as well – was also passed on and probably influenced the development of a Christian doctrine of the Trinity. What is now new is the equating of one of the two angels with Jesus Christ and the other with the Holy Spirit.

In the Ascension of Isaiah, an apocalypse which was assembled out of various (pre-Christian-Jewish and Christian) parts at the earliest in the 2nd century, the „Lord of glory," the „other glorious one" and – as a third – „the angel of the Holy Spirit" were worshipped; thus they are entitled to divinity. Yet Jesus Christ and the Spirit are nevertheless subordinated to „God as such": „And I saw how my Lord worshipped and the angel of the Holy Spirit and how both together praised God."[95]

Likewise in Christian interpolations in the *Ethiopic Book of Enoch*, which was probably compiled in the 2nd century B.C., next to the aged one, God, „another, whose form (was) like the appearance of a man, and his countenance

---

[95] 9.40; cf. the contexts (Christian interpolation) 9.1-6: „[1] And he carried me into the atmosphere of the seventh heaven. ... [3] And I asked the angel who was with me, and spoke: Who is that one who forbade me, and who is this one who permits me to ascend? [4] And he spoke to me: He who forbade you (it) is the one who (is set) above the hymns of praise of the sixth heaven, [5] and he who gave you permission is your Lord, God, Christ the Lord, who on earth would be called Jesus, but you cannot hear his name until you ascend out of your body. [6] And he let me ascend into the seventh heaven, and there I saw a wonderful light and angels beyond counting" (eds. Hennecke and Schneemelcher, *Neutestamentliche Apokryphen in deutscher Übersetzung*, Vol. II [Tübingen, [5]1989], pp. 557, 558).

9.27-40: „[27] And I saw one standing there whose glory exceeded everything, and his glory was great and wonderful. [28] And after I caught sight of him, all the righteous ones that I saw and all the angels that I saw came to him, and first Adam, Abel and Seth and all of the righteous ones went up, worshipped him. ... [31] Then the angel who was guiding me spoke to me: Worship him! And I worshipped and sang hymns of praise. [32] And the angel spoke to me: It is the Lord of all glory that you have seen. [33] And while (the angel) was still speaking, I saw another glorious one who was like him, and the righteous ones went up, worshipped and sang hymns of praise, and I too sang hymns of praise with them, but my glory did not transform itself according to their appearance. [34] And after that the angel went up and worshipped. [35] And I saw the Lord and the second angel, and they stood, however the other one that I had seen was on the left-hand side of my Lord. [36] And I asked: Who is this one? And he spoke to me: Worship him, for this is the angel of the Holy Spirit that speaks (*Eth.*: has spoken) through you and the other righteous ones. ... [39] Then my Lord came to me, and the angel of the Spirit and spoke: See how it is given to you to behold God and how for your sake power has been given to the angel with you.

[40] And I saw how my Lord worshipped and the angel of the Holy Spirit and how both together praised God" (eds. Hennecke and Schneemelcher, op. cit., pp. 558, 559).

full of goodness like (that) of a holy angel," is seen in a vision[96]; according to the context, Jesus is meant. Nothing is mentioned about a „Spirit" except in a later (but very vague) passage that says of the Son of Man: „And in him resides the spirit of wisdom and the spirit which imparts insight, and the spirit of the teaching and power and the spirit of those who have passed away into righteousness."[97]

A Christian insertion in the *Apocalypse of Elchasai*, composed around 100 B.C., speaks of two huge angels, one with a male and one with a female form; „the male is the Son of God, the female is characterized as the Holy Spirit."[98]

The Christian apocalypse *„Shepherd of Hermas,"* which originated in Rome around 150, speaks of a „glorious man," the „Son of God," and suffers another „six ... glorious angels"[99] to stand next to him, but six angels that are subordinated to him and are not to be understood as the putting together of a third angel hypostasis.

Conceptions of this kind, which had come over from early Judaism, must have been widespread. In any event, the later Alexandrian theologians *Clement* and *Origen* of Alexandria still remind us of this tradition. *Clement* († before 215) characterizes the Logos as an angel that is incarnated in Jesus,[100] and *Origen* († c. 250) interprets the two cherubim on the Ark of the Covenant as the Word of God and the Spirit.[101]

---

[96] XLVI 1-8 (ed. Siegbert Uhlig, *Das äthiopische Henochbuch. Jüdische Schriften aus hellenistisch-römischer Zeit*, Vol. V, fasc. 6 [Gütersloh, 1984], p. 587); cf. XLVII 1-4; XLVIII 1-10.

[97] XLVI 3 (ed. Uhlig, op. cit., p. 592).

[98] In a fragment according to St. Hippolytus, ref. 9.13, 1-3 (ed. Hennecke and Schneemelcher, *Neutestamentliche Apokryphen in deutscher Übersetzung*, Vol. II, op. cit., p. 621).

[99] *Sim.* IX 12.8 (ed. Norbert Brox, *Der Hirt des Hermas* in *Kommentar zu den Apostolischen Vätern*, ed. N. Brox u.a., Vol. 7 [Göttingen, 1991], p. 413).

[100] *Der Pädagoge (Paidagogos,* c. 203), I 59,1: (The Lord, God himself, was through Moses our teacher) „Then who could teach us with greater love than he? Now, earlier the older tribe had an older covenant, ..., *and the Logos was an angel* (Exod. 3.2), to the newer and younger tribe, on the other hand, a newer and younger covenant has be given, and the Logos is become flesh, ..., and the mysterious angel Jesus is born" (translated from the German in: K.-H. Ohlig, *Christologie I [Texte zur Theologie, Dogmatik,* Vol IV.1], [Graz, Wien, Köln, 1989], in the following cited as: TzT 4.1; No. 79).

[101] *Kommentar zum Römerbrief,* in Rom. 3.25 (ed. Theresia Heither, *Origenes: Commentarii in epistulam ad Romanos / Römerbriefkommentar* in Latin and German [*Fontes Christiani;* Vol. 2/2], [Freiburg im Breisgau u.a., 1992], pp. 119-121): „Cherubim, namely, translated into our language, means ‚abundance of knowledge.' We can, however, only speak of the abundance of knowledge in that one of whom the apostle says: ‚In whom are hid all the treasures of wisdom and knowledge' (Col. 2.3). Surely he is saying that of the Word of God. However, he also writes the same thing of the Holy Spirit with the words: ‚But God hath revealed them unto us by his Spirit: for the Spirit searcheth all things, yea, the deep things of God' (1 Cor. 2.10). In my opinion this is an indication that on the mercy seat, that is in the

Thus, in the theology affected by Jewish-Christian influences in the 2nd century either no Trinitarian thinking or only a very sparing use of binitarian or Trinitarian mythological angel motifs, now Christianized, can be established. These traditions could also have developed in quite different ways. The real breakthrough to a doctrine of the binity or of the Trinity only first occurred in for the most part Hellenistic conceptions, such as those that predominate in the early Christian apologists and in Gnosticism.

4.3 Hellenistic-Christian Traditions

4.3.1 The Profession of Faith in Jesus as „God"

In Hellenistic Christianity Jesus Christ is – in connection with impulses from the New Testament – acknowledged as the incarnated Logos. *Ignatius* of Antioch († between 109 and 117) calls him „God in the shape of a man"[102] or „our God, Jesus, the Christ."[103] For this reason it can be assumed that – although he does not explicitly write this – in the few passages in which he strings together God, Christ and Spirit triadically,[104] he at least had latently binitarian ideas. Similarly, in the *Second Epistle of St. Clement*, a text probably composed between 130 and 150, one can „perhaps sift out the following ideas: Jesus Christ was spirit; he became flesh. ... What it [the Epistle of St. Clement] offers is, so to speak, the ecclesiastical standard."[105]

Hence the only thing that can be inferred from these few texts is that the godhood of Jesus Christ is being expressed. The consequences of this view for the conceptions of God were not pursued. This does, however, occur in the works of a series of cultivated Hellenistic Christians who wanted in their writings to defend Christianity against reproaches from the heathen side – the „apologists" (*apologia* = „defense").

---

soul of Jesus, the Word of God, and that is His only begotten Son, and the Holy Spirit always reside. Precisely this is shown by the two cherubim placed upon the mercy seat."
[102] *Ad. Eph.* 19.3 (German: TzT 4.1, No. 43).
[103] Ibid. 18.2 (German: ibid.).
[104] E.g. *ad Magn.* 13.1 („in the Son and in the Father and in the Spirit"); cf. ibid. 13.2; *ad Eph.* 18.2.
[105] Klaus Wengst in his introduction to *2 Clem.* in *Didache (Apostellehre), Barnabasbrief, Zweiter Klemensbrief, Schrift an Diognet.*, introd., ed., trans., and annotated by Klaus Wengst (*Schriften des Urchristentums*, Part 2), (Darmstadt, 1984), p. 229.

4.3.2 The Development by the Apologists of a Doctrine of the Binity

For the apologists, Jesus is „God" or „Son of the highest God,"[106] for whom the title of Logos from the prologue to the Gospel according to St. John (John 1) soon prevailed. Thus it was soon necessary that one consciously reflect that – when one spoke of „God" – one was dealing with „God *and his Logos*." For this concept of God, however, there was a literary model, the Jewish theologian and contemporary of Jesus, *Philo* of Alexandria.[107] This is why the most important of the apologists refers to his comments, *Justin Martyr* († c. 165). The latter was influenced by a popular form of middle Platonism and the Stoics, wrote eight works, three of which (two apologies and a dialogue with a Jew named Trypho) are extant.

Jesus is for him the incarnated Logos, and that is „God." Thus, however, it is clear for *Justin Martyr* – and also the unequivocal teaching of the Holy Scripture (the Old Testament)[108] – that in God there is a „plural";[109] for the Logos is begotten by God, „and it is, the Begotten One, in terms of its number, a different one than the Begetter."[110]

Like *Philo*, *Justin Martyr* also refers to the Old Testament story of God's visit to Abraham.[111] Abraham „lifted up his eyes and looked, and, lo, three men stood by him,"[112] of which two are – according to the following chapter Genesis 19 – two angels. Oddly, however, in his explanations *Justin Martyr* speaks only of „the" angel, of the Logos; he no longer mentions the second one, which means that the Spirit was still of no relevance for his theology. It is true that he names him in his First Apology: „Now, that we are not godless, since we worship the Creator of this universe ... – what reasonable person would not admit that? And that we have furthermore placed ... Jesus Christ ..., whom we have recognized as the Son of the true God, in the second position and that we honor the prophetic Spirit in the third position, that we will demonstrate."[113] According to *Justin Martyr* even *Plato* had taught a threefold structuring of the divine.[114] Nevertheless, as *Herbert Vorgrimler* correctly interprets: „The Spirit is only mentioned in passing."[115] Thus *Justin Martyr* talks almost exclusively of God and his Logos. The latter, however, is subordinated to the quintessential God, to the Father who is too great and

---

[106] Aristides of Athens, *Apologie* (between 117 and 138, German: TzT 4.1, No. 52).
[107] Cf. above 27-29.
[108] Gen. 3.22: „And the Lord God said, Behold, the man is become as one of us."
[109] *Dialog mit dem Juden Tryphon* CXXIX.2 (German: TzT 4.1, No. 55).
[110] Ibid. CXXIX.4 (German: ibid.).
[111] Gen. 18.
[112] Gen. 18.2.
[113] *First Apol.* 13 (German: TzT 4.1, No. 53); cf. ibid. p. 60.
[114] *Apol.* I 60.
[115] Herbert Vorgrimler, *Gotteslehre I* (*Texte zur Theologie, Dogmatik, 2.1*; hereinafter cited as: TzT 2.1), (Graz, Wien, Köln, 1989), Introduction to No. 84.

distant and „remains always above the heavens, never appeared to anyone and never associated with anyone in his own person,"[116] about whom no one dares to declare that „the Creator and Father of the universe has left everything that is above heaven and has appeared in one small corner of the earth."[117]

Here it becomes clear that the Biblical monotheism has been enriched with Greek motifs. God is so very immutable and eternal that He Himself cannot act. As in early Judaism, that requires a lesser divine force, the Logos. The Logos takes over the mediating function in creation and now also – the Christian expansion – the Incarnation in Jesus.

However, with this step a tension results between monotheism and the number „two." *Justin Martyr* again solves this problem by referring to a conception of *Philo*'s which also defines the train of thought in the prologue to the Gospel according to St. John. The Logos was „before all Creation in Him," the Father, and was first begotten „as He in the beginning created and ordered everything through it."[118] *In the beginning* is a reference to Gen. 1.1: „In the beginning God created the heaven and the earth," and means that the Logos first appeared as an important figure separate from God at the beginning of the creation process: „Before all creatures God begot out of himself a reasonable force which ... is called the glory of the Lord, another time Son, then wisdom, sometimes angel, sometimes God, sometimes Lord and Logos."[119]

Justin Martyr therefore, like *Philo* and John 1, distinguishes between the Logos that is eternally in God and identical with Him, and the Logos that appeared out of Him „in the beginning" – an attempt to preserve the monotheism despite the number „two." However, this attempt only succeeds verbally insofar as the „Logos" that appeared out of God in the beginning is asserted to be eternally identical with God. In substance, however, nothing has been settled: the Logos identical with God is only another word for God, who indeed *is* Thought; that which is begotten out of Him „in the beginning" has in fact a beginning and is God only in a lesser form. Here two quite different figures are being designated with „Logos." In any case, however, a term thus seemed to have been found that appeared to reconcile *Justin Martyr*'s de facto ditheism with the inherited monotheism.

The task of the Logos is – in accordance with what was taken over from early Judaism – to constitute the world immanently; it is – in accordance with its roots – the cosmic and impersonal Hellenistic God. Thus in a „Petition for the Christians" (between 176 and 180) the apologist *Athenagoras* of Athens, whose conception of God is generally speaking the same as that of *Justin Martyr*, also characterizes the Logos as „exemplary (for the structures of the cosmos, K.-H. O.) thought and creative force."[120]

---

[116] *Dial.* LVI 1 (TzT 4.1, No. 55).
[117] Ibid. LX 2 (TzT 4.1, No. 55).
[118] *Apol.* II 5 (6) (German: TzT 4.1, No. 54).
[119] *Dial.* LXI 1 (German: TzT 4.1, No. 55).
[120] *Petition* 10 (German: TzT 4.1, No. 58).

The cosmic divinity of the Logos does however acquire a certain „personal" character in all the apologists because by means of Christianity the creative Logos was now also incarnated in Jesus and thus connected with him. But since God, according to the evidence of the New Testament, is the Father of Jesus and the latter is his son, this is joined by the anthropologically filled motifs of this figurative language, hence by the begetting and the being begotten. According to *Justin Martyr* and according to *Athenagoras* („the Son of God is the Logos"[121]), the „emergence" of the Logos „in the beginning" is also understood as a begetting by the father. A binitarian doctrine is now firmly established, although it exhibits fundamental theological weaknesses, insofar as the Logos is understood as a second god subordinate to the first god and only existing separately since the „beginning."

4.3.3 The Reestablishment of Monotheism by Syrian Theologians

In the extended area of Syria, which reached from the Mediterranean Sea to Mesopotamia, the majority of the population was Semitic. Even in the western part centered around Antioch (today Antakya in southeastern Turkey) where the Greek language was widespread, Semitic thought developed its influence. In a way somewhat comparable to the Jewish understanding, history plays a greater role here. For this reason the Syrian Christians had no „need" for a Hellenistic world principle, and Jesus was important for them because he had „proved" himself to God in his actions. Although they also called him the Son of God, understood within this was that God had adopted him as son on the basis of his obedience unto the Cross.

That is why in this area no necessity was felt for conceiving of the Logos as a divine creative principle and as the subject of the Incarnation. As was demonstrated especially in the 3rd century, a pure monotheism („monarchianism") was advocated. When there was talk of Logos or Spirit, they interpreted them as „powers" (*dynameis*) – „dynamistic monarchianism" – or as different manifestations or modes (*modi*) of the *one* God – „modalism," „Sabellianism," „Patripassianism."[122]

This thinking was already in the offing in the 2nd century. Although the apologist *Tatian* of Syria and the bishop *Theophilos* of Antioch (both 2nd half of the 2nd century), who was the first to use the word „*trias*"[123] (trinity), also took over the way of speaking about God and his Logos stemming from *Philo*, in terms of content the schemes were the same as those used by *Justin Martyr*.

However, they interpret this scheme in a new, specifically „Syrian" way: according to *Tatian* the Syrian God Himself was already the „Lord of All Things who at the same time is the hypostasis (the original ground) of the

---

[121] Ibid.
[122] Cf. 4.6 below.
[123] *Ad. Autol.* II 15.

universe."[124] Therefore there was no need for a Logos to take over this function although it did then participate in the Creation. The Logos emerged from God in the beginning „and was the Father's first-born work: we know that it is the beginning of the world."[125] Thus, because the Logos has a temporal beginning, it is viewed as a „work" of God which arose „through an act of God's will"; before the beginning, „namely at a time at which there was still no Creation, the Lord of All Things" was „alone."[126]

Theophilos of Antioch admittedly also writes: „And thus God with his wisdom begot the word which he bore enclosed within his bosom," and this Logos – a still nonspecific terminology – „is the spirit of God, the principle (of all things)."[127] But he continues: „When however God wanted to create all of the things that he had concluded to create, He begot this word *as something pronounced*, the first-born of any creature."[128]

In other words, although the Logos „in the beginning" emerged from God, became the mediator of the Creation and was combined with Jesus, it is still a „work" or a „creature," notwithstanding its being the first and noblest work. This interpretation of the Logos, which was still being advocated more than a century later by *Arius*, a theologian educated in Antioch, basically draws a logical conclusion from the Logos schema known since *Philo*: If the Logos – as a separate entity – has a temporal beginning, it is to be numbered among the creatures; it is, however, ascribed a high status and it stands quite near to God, but without calling into question the monotheism or monarchianism.

4.3.4 Decisive Impulses from Gnosticism

Even before the turn of the era around the Mediterranean there arose a new religious movement which spread in a parallel fashion to Christianity and coexisted with – and partially in – it: Gnosticism. According to Gnosticism salvation occurs through „knowing" (gnosis), through the knowledge of „where we were, whither we have been cast, whither we are hurrying, whereby we have been saved, what birth is, what rebirth."[129] For a long time this religion was known only as a heresy within Christianity. Only in this century did one discover that it exists in additional forms and should be conceived of as a specific understanding of life in late antiquity which was combined with various religious traditions whose mythic material it used to express its own views. This thesis is also confirmed by the non-Christian *Corpus Hermeticum*, a

---

[124] *Address to the Greeks* 5.1 (German: TzT 4.1, No. 59)

[125] *Address to the Greeks* 5.1, 2 (German: TzT 4.1, No. 59).

[126] Ibid. 5.1 (German: ibid.).

[127] *Ad Autol.* II 10 (German: TzT 4.1, No. 60).

[128] Ibid. II 22 (German: ibid., emphasis mine, K.-H. O.).

[129] The Gnostic Theodotus (2nd century A.D.) as recorded in Clement of Alexandria, *Against Theodotus* 78.2 (SCh 23, 1948), p. 202.

collection of writings whose central figure is the Greek god Hermes, and by the discoveries of *Nag Hammadi*.[130] Since then the conviction has prevailed that Gnosticism represents an independent religion of early antiquity which, although it parasitically[131] makes use of outside religious traditions and also develops different forms of organization, is nevertheless a unity. What is fundamental is a negative valuation of concrete reality, a world pessimism; man sees himself as a stranger cast into this world. The fact that he suffers from it shows, however, that deep down he is destined for a better reality and bears it within himself. He is thus split within himself and fluctuates between good and evil, between a life in relation to the spirit and a life in relation to the material world.

This ethical alternative, however, is grounded in the reality of the world and of mankind and thus becomes an *ontological dualism*: „The image of God is dualistic: Opposite the upper, ultramundane, spiritual and good God, his domain (the Pleroma) and its inhabitants (eons), on the one side, stand the incapable, ignorant creator of the world (Demiurge) and his followers (archons, planetary spirits, etc.), matter, the cosmos and the world of man, on the other. ... Thus for the Gnostics the world is a product of misfortune and weakness. The upper God need not answer for it."[132]

The creation of the world reality is the result of a series of emanations, at the beginning of which either – according to the more moderate viewpoint – the fundamentally one and good God stood, but one of the lesser figures proceeding from him has – through blindness, misunderstanding and sin – turned away from his origin and now embodies the evil opposing principle; or there are more radical forms of Gnosticism in which the opposing principle is not an emanation, but just as original as the good God. The evil principle – or the rival god – becomes, according to Gnostic myths, the creator of the world, the *Demiurge*. He „creates" everything by mixing what is spiritual and full of light with the material and the dark; human souls are banished by him into matter. Thus the world reality is marked by the coexistence of good and evil; the Gnostic longs to be freed from the material circumstances which limit him and motivate him to be evil.

Because the good God faced a world in which the good, spiritual and full of light were combined with the evil, material and dark, and he himself, in order

---

[130] In 1945/46 in the vicinity of the Upper Egyptian district town of Nag Hammadi farmers found an earthenware jug with 13 codices of papyrus written around the year 400. They contained writings (from the 2nd to the 4th century) representing hermetic and other Gnostic lines of thought, but above all they also contained Christian-Gnostic writings from which it would almost be possible to compile an alternative New Testament.

[131] According to Norbert Brox's „Einführung. Die Epoche der Gnosis," in: *Irenäus von Lyon. Epideixis, Adversus haereses. Darlegung der Apostolischen Verkündigung. Gegen die Häresien I*, trans. and introd. Norbert Brox, Fontes Christiani, Vol. 8/1 (Freiburg, Basel, Wien, 1993), p. 8.

[132] Norbert Brox, ibid., pp. 9, 10.

to keep himself from being soiled, could have no contact with it, one imagined between God and the world a region of the *Pleroma*, the „abundance," of intermediary spiritual entities who are derived in complicated successions – here there are a large number of fantastic myths – from God. One of the eons takes on the task of bringing to the souls that have been scattered into human bodies and have fallen into misunderstanding the knowledge of the true overall scheme of things and thereby their redemption. In the Christian variation this figure of redemption is Jesus Christ.

Young Christianity's attempt to come to terms with Gnosticism was so difficult because the Hellenistic Christians to a large extent thought and felt like the Gnostics. In this way Gnostic views were able to spread in Christianity. Above all it seemed to make sense that an abundance of „divine" emanations had to mediate between God as such and the world, so that „God alone" was no longer sufficient for the explanation of the creation of the world – although the Christians ascribed it, not to an evil principle, but to God – and for the explanation of redemption; additional heavenly figures were necessary.

A few examples should make this thinking clear:

Example 1: The Odes of Solomon

The Odes of Solomon („Solomon" stands for Jesus Christ), which were written in the first quarter of the second century and thus still in „New Testament times," are a kind of Christian-Gnostic song book; the occasion of its creation were probably Col. 3.16 and Eph. 5.19, where there is talk about „psalms, hymns and spiritual songs" of the Christians. In many of the 42 songs it is a question of the gnosis and words of truth which flow down out of the heavenly world. The „mouth of the Lord (is) the true word ... and the gate of his light. And the Supreme One gave it to his eons. ... For the speed of the word cannot be told. ... And the eons spoke through it (sc. the word), one to the other. ... For the tent of the word (cf. John 1.14) is the (Son of) Man, and its (sc. the word's) truth is love."[133] Obviously, the gnosis is imparted from God through the eons, and the word dwelled in the Son of Man.

Similar thoughts can be found in Ode 19, which also incorporates the Spirit: „The cup of milk approached me, and I drank it in the sweetness of the mildness of the Lord. The Son is the cup, and he who was milked, the Father, and he who milked him, the spiritual power of holiness." A few verses further on an allusion is made to the Incarnation: „The womb of the Virgin conceived, and she became pregnant and bore. And the Virgin became a mother in great love and had labor pains and bore a son."[134] Or the following: „The Father of the gnosis is the word of the gnosis. He who has created *sophia* (wisdom, K.-H. O.) is wiser than his works. ... Because He is, He is immortal; the Pleroma

---

[133] Ode 12, vv. 3-12 (German in: *Oden Salomos*, trans. and introd. Michael Lanke [Fontes Christiani, Vol. 19], [Freiburg, Basel, Wien, et.al., 1995]), pp. 136-138.

[134] Ode 19, vv. 1-7 (German: ibid., pp. 153, 154).

of eons is their father. He allows it so that He may appear to those who are his, that they would recognize him who created them."[135]

There is no fundamental dualism in the *Odes of Solomon*; even the Creation is the work of God. But between it and the world is an abundance of eons, among which are the word and the spirit or *sophia*. Without them, neither the world reality nor the redemption from lies and misunderstanding can be explained. If Jesus is really the Redeemer, he must – it goes without saying – be the incarnation of a heavenly hypostasis.

Example 2: The Valentinian Gnosis

These patterns of thought are even more clearly marked, for instance, in *Valentinian Gnosticism*, whose system is described by the bishop *Irenaeus* of Lyons († c. 202) in his work, „Against the Heresies." These Gnostics enumerated an abundance of emanations: From one „unnamable dyad (duality)" emanated a second dyad, which in turn produced as fruit the „Logos and *zoe* (life), *anthropos* and *ecclesia*." From the Logos and *zoe* emanated „ten powers," and so forth. „Christ, however, was not emanated by the eons in the Pleroma, but by the mother excluded from it (sc. the Pleroma)," and the „holy *pneuma* was emanated by the Truth." It goes on like this. „Speaking of Jesus he (Valentinus, K.-H. O.) one time says that he was emanated by the (eon) separated from their mother."[136] Redemption is also only conceivable here as the reporting of knowledge from the intermediary realm of the Pleroma through the mediation of lesser hypostases emanated from God.

Example 3: The Gospel of the Truth

The system of the „Gospel of the Truth" (2nd/3rd century) „looks like this: The highest God is the Father of the Truth, which is not created, but is without beginning. Its place of abode is the Pleroma. The Father brings forth his Son Logos, who is also called Jesus Christ and Savior. Then the Father creates the universe, the eons. They are all in the Pleroma. ... Only the Logos knows the Father. The eons can only recognize the Father through the mediation of the Logos. However, since the eons on their own look for the Father and do not find him, they become uneasy, anxious and frightened. Their cognitive faculties are paralyzed. ... The *planê* arises, the misunderstanding that does not know the Father. The misunderstanding brings forth matter and forms out of it the temporal world and the bodies of the first men. ... In the lower world envy and conflict prevail. ... Seen from the reality of the Father the entire lower world is a void, only appearance. ... This defect will be removed by the Logos at the end of time. It comes out of the Pleroma in the upper world of the eons and reveals to the eons, whose form it assumes, the knowledge of the Father. Then it descends as Jesus Christ and Savior into the lower world, assumes a body made of flesh. ... Misunderstanding, the ruler of the lower world, feels

---

[135] Ode 7, vv. 7, 8, 11, and 12 (German: ibid., pp. 110, 111); cf. Ode 13, v. 2.

[136] Iren., *Adv. haer.* I, 11.1 (German: loc. cit., pp. 207, 209).

threatened by him, and he is nailed to the Cross, so that he dies ‚for many.' He then dons his immortality and returns into the Pleroma. ..."[137]

In the text of the „Gospel of the Truth" an account is given of God and the Logos: „The gospel of the Truth is rejoicing for those who have received grace from the Father of the Truth; that they recognize Him through the power of the word (Logos) which has come from the Pleroma: that word which was in the thought and in the *nous* (understanding, K.-H. O.) of the Father – that is the one they call the ‚Savior' – ... That is the gospel ... which he revealed to those who are perfect, the secret mystery, Jesus Christ; through this one He has enlightened those who are in darkness through forgetting. ... Therefore the *planê* (= the misunderstanding) was angry with him; it persecuted him. ... He was nailed to the Cross. ... After he had filled (removed) the defect, he dissolved the external appearance. His external appearance is the world in which he had served. ..."[138]

Example 4: The Pistis Sophia

The Coptic *Pistis Sophia* presents texts that date back to the time of the later Gnostics in the 3rd century. In the first part, the resurrected Christ converses, twelve years after his death, with Mary and with John; in terms of content, it is a question of the „fall and the redemption of the Pistis Sophia, one of the many figures in the Gnostic world of redemption."[139]

„*The resurrected Jesus speaks to his disciples*

7. ‚And when I had set off for the world, I came into the middle of the archons ... of the spheres ... and had the form of Gabriel, the angel ... of the eons ...; and the archons ... of the eons ... did not recognize me, rather ... they thought that I was the angel ... Gabriel. Now it happened that, when I had come into the middle of the archons ... of the eons ..., I looked down upon the world ... of mankind, by order ... of the primal mystery. ... I found Elizabeth, the mother of John the Baptist, before she had conceived him, and I sowed a power into her. ... That power is now found in the body ... of John ...

8. ... It now happened that after that I looked by order ... of the primal mystery ... down upon the world of mankind and found Mary, who is called ‚my mother' in accordance ... with her material ... body ...; I spoke with her in ... the form ... of Gabriel, and when she had turned up towards me I drove into her the primal power which I had taken from Barbelo[140] ... And at the place of

---

[137] Summary of the editors, from: „Evangelium der Wahrheit," trans. and annot. Martin Krause and Kurt Rudolph, in: C. Adresen (ed.), *Die Gnosis*, vol. 2: *Koptische und Mandäische Quellen* (Zurich, Stuttgart, 1971), pp. 64-66.

[138] TzT 4.1, No. 67.

[139] Gerhard Schneider in: „Evangelia infantiae apocrypha. Apocryphe Kindheitsevangelien," trans. and introd. Gerhard Schneider, Fontes Christiani, Vol. 18 (Freiburg, Basel, Wien, et. al., 1995), p. 84.

[140] Barbelo is in some Gnostic myths the first (female) emanation from God and herself a kind of Gnostic maternal deity.

the soul ... I drove into her the power which I had taken from the great Sabaoth the Good'."

In Section 61 there is also talk of the Spirit that, because of its similarity to Jesus, Mary took for a ghost and tied to the bed. When Jesus returned to the house with Joseph and Mary, „(we [as Mary recounts, K.-H. O.]) found the Spirit ... bound to the bed. And we looked at you (Jesus, K.-H. O.) and him and found you resembling him; and the one bound to the bed was freed, he embraced you and kissed you, also you kissed him, and you became one ...".[141]

The variety of Gnostic hypostases, one of which then – in the Christian versions – was incarnated in Jesus, is almost incalculable. Nevertheless, there is also already in them a certain preference for the number three: „Over and over again we primarily encounter the three. It is after all the expression of plurality. ... Often one takes as a starting point ... the pagan conception of god father, god mother and divine child."[142] In what follows, *A. Böhlig* enumerates a series of Gnostic texts in which different divine trinities are emphasized,[143] and comes to the conclusion that „from that point, it is just one more step to the God-Son-Spirit trinity."[144]

The Gnostic texts with their constructions of heavenly emanations mediating between God and the world seem abstruse to us today. But their dissemination in the Hellenistic society around the Mediterranean may indicate that they corresponded to the mentality at the time. It was taken for granted that with the assumption of the ultimate principle of Good, that is God, He himself could neither create the evil world nor bring about redemption. It seemed to be *a logical necessity* to assume such lesser, divine intermediary entities, in order to be able to explain the reality of the world and hopes of mankind for redemption.

These patterns of thought were also shared by many Christians, which is why Gnosticism could spread so widely in the Church. The eventually victorious theological struggle against Gnosticism was directed towards two objectives: *On the one hand*, in time the impact began to be felt of the Biblical conception of the Creation, according to which the world was created by God and was – before the Fall of Man – good; an ontological or cosmic dualism was rejected in favor of an ethical dualism (evil is a consequence of the action of man). This, however, could not prevent the former dualism from continuing to have a latent effect and in Christianity – often to this day – the „earthly things," body, woman, sexuality, material possessions and the self-determination of one's life, were viewed as inferior; the „perfect" Christian had to live „spiritually," ideal-

---

[141] *Pistis Sophia* (German in: ibid., pp. 327-329).

[142] Alexander Böhlig, *Gnosis und Synkretismus. Gesammelte Aufsätze zur spätantiken Religionsgeschichte Teil 1* (Wissenschaftliche Untersuchungen zum Neuen Testament; 47), (Tübingen, 1989), p. 18.

[143] Ibid., pp. 18-20.

[144] Ibid., p. 20; cf. by the same author, „Triade und Trinität in den Schriften von Nag Hammadi," in *Gnosis und Synkretismus*, loc. cit., pp. 289-311.

typically embodied in monasticism, emergent since the 3rd century out of precisely these motifs, with its renunciation of sexuality, material possessions and a will of one's own.

On the other hand, the Church theologians fought *the abstruse variety* of heavenly hypostases and declared these to be „mythology." One may take as an example *Irenaeus*, who in his books *Against the Heresies* – in which he means above all the Gnostics – even makes fun of them for making virtually every symbolic name in Biblical texts into hypostases of their own emanated from God: „Oh dear, oh dear! One has to let out a groan at such concocting of names and the insolence with which he (an unnamed Gnostic, K.-H. O.) has, without blushing, sought out names for his cock-and-bull stories."[145]

Irenaeus engages in polemics against the Gnostics who, for example, pick out of the prologue to the Gospel according to St. John the notion that eight emanations (an *ogdoas*) ensue from God by declaring the terms occurring there („beginning," „word," „life," etc.) to be separate hypostases.[146] He insists that John is only speaking of *one* Logos, which has emerged from the Father and been incarnated in Jesus Christ.[147] „So understand, you fools, that Jesus ... and no one else is the Logos of God. ... If the Logos of the Father that descended is also that which ascended ..., then John was not speaking about a different one and also not about an ogdaos."[148] Or in another passage: „Since the Spirit therefore ... has come down and the Son of God, ... who is also the Word (Logos) of the Father, when time became fulfilled ... is in a man become flesh, ... (for that reason) all the teachings of those who have invented the ogdoadis (octads), tetradis (tetrads) and (other) illusionary figures and thought-up subdivisions are exposed as lies."[149]

The argumentation is thus *against the escalation in hypostatization*s that the Gnostics had carried out, *but not against the basic idea as such:* Irenaeus merely reduces the number to the Logos (and the Spirit). The conceptual framework, however, that for the explanation of Creation and redemption it is not enough to refer to God, but that divine mediating figures are necessary, applies to him as well. „The criticism of Irenaeus simply comes down to reducing the multitude of divine eons emerging from God the Father to one divine Logos-Son who is begotten from the Father and becomes flesh in the earthly Jesus. This reduction takes place within the same basic mutually presupposed and acknowledged scheme."[150] Quite obviously the reasons both for the retaining of the myth and for its (quantitative) reduction are to be

---

[145] *Adv. haer.* I, 11.4 (German translation from: Fontes Christiani, Vol. 8/1, loc. cit., p. 211).

[146] *Adv. haer.* I, 8.5-9.2.

[147] Ibid. 9.2.

[148] Ibid. 9.2 (German translation from: Fontes Christiani, Vol. 8/1, loc. cit., pp. 191, 193).

[149] *Adv. haer.* III, 17.4 (German translation from: Irenäus von Lyon, *Adversus haereses. Gegen die Häresien III*, trans. and introd. Norbert Brox [Fontes Christiani, Vol. 8/3], [Freiburg, Basel, Wien, et. al., 1995], p. 217).

[150] M. Werner, *Die Entstehung des christlichen Dogmas* (Tübingen, ²1941), p. 561.

sought in the Hellenistic-Christian Christology: The „principle of exchange" made it necessary to see in Jesus the incarnated God – otherwise his soteriological significance could not be absorbed – and his importance would likewise be „damaged" or relativized by the acceptance of numerous further hypostatizations – a limitation to the Christological hypostasis (and that of the Spirit) was soteriologically imperative. This was why there could be *no overcoming* of Gnosticism, for instance, in the sense that the original vis-à-vis of God and Jesus would have been reestablished.

This observation is also true for the other „early Catholic" writers who after the turn of the 3rd century developed their conceptions about God and Creation/ redemption in the confrontation with Gnosticism: for *Tertullian* in the West, *Clement* and *Origen* of Alexandria in the East of the Church at that time. In their conceptions Gnosticism is not overcome, but merely „Christianized" through the rejection of a *fundamental* dualism (but not of a dualistic attitude towards life) and through the limitation of the hypostases between God and the world to the number two: the Logos/Son and the Spirit.

Thus the Gnostic mentality, which in general illustrates the Hellenistic thinking and feeling at this time in an exaggerated but exemplary manner, is an important impetus in causing the Christian way of thinking about God to grow more strongly Trinitarian. The one good God alone could not explain the coming into being of Creation and redemption; *at the least* Logos/Son and Spirit – and from Christological motivations: *they alone* – were indispensable for the solving of this problem.

4.4 Eternal Monotheism and the „Trinity" in Salvation History

Irenaeus of Lyons († c. 202), a native of Asia Minor and writing in Greek, and *Tertullian* of Carthage, the most important formulator of the developing Latin theology, represent a new stage of development in the formation of Trinitarian thinking before and after the turn of the third century. What is „new" in their case is on the one hand the stronger position of the Holy Spirit, which first resulted from the confrontation with the Gnostics insofar as they reduced their inflationary doctrine of emanation to the economically, that is, the salvation-historically necessary minimum, but then also as a result of the stabilization that had meanwhile occurred in the essential parts of the New Testament canon,[151] whereby the – apparently – triadic passages, especially the order to baptize in Matt. 28.19, developed a normative force. Another „new" developmental advance consists in the way *Irenaeus* and *Tertullian* take over the already existing traditional concepts and intellectual frameworks and consider them *in terms of their systematic content*. They take up the Biblical monotheism and the apologists' speculation on the Logos – expanded to

---

[151] Cf. by the present author, *Die theologische Begründung des neutestamentlichen Kanons in der alten Kirche* (Düsseldorf, 1972), e.g., p. 43.

include the Spirit – and attempt to combine them. *As a result they combine an inner-godly or immanent monotheism with an „economic" Trinity which first came into being with the Creation and redemption from the „beginning."*

For *Irenaeus* God is an absolute unity, far from all differentiation[152]; in opposition to the Gnostic dualism He is also the cosmic God „who embraces everything."[153] Although there are the Word and the Spirit in God, they are contained within him eternally[154] and are identical with him; *Irenaeus* thinks in monarchian terms as far as God is concerned and has no immanent conception of the Trinity.[155]

When *Karlmann Beyschlag* interprets this being-within-God of the Son and Spirit in the sense of a „perpetual coexistence,"[156] he mistakes – as does the translation by *Norbert Brox* – the intentions of *Irenaeus*.[157] For the apologists as well as for the Gnostics, God – before the beginning of the emanations – is, regarded for himself, all one, wherein Biblical monotheism has been linked with the Greek thought of the simple being of God. According to *A. von Harnack*, „Irenaeus does not want the term ‚Logos' to be understood in such a way that the Logos would be the inner reason or the spoken word of God: God is a simple entity ..."[158]

Like the apologists, but against the Gnostics, *Irenaeus* emphasizes God's being the creator and in doing so shifts the Creation into the vicinity of God; here the soteriological motives for seeing to it that the unity of the Creation and God is not dualistically destroyed are decisive. At the same time, however, he – like the Gnostics and Hellenistic thought as a whole – cannot abandon divine

---

[152] Cf. *adv. haer.* II, 13.3 (German translation from: Irenäus von Lyon, *Adversus haereses. Gegen die Häresien II*, trans. and introd. Norbert Brox [Fontes Christiani, Vol. 8/2], [Freiburg, Basel, Wien, et. al., 1993], pp. 95, 96): „The Father of all things ... is simple and not composite ..., since He is all understanding, all spirit, all feeling, all thought, all reason, all ears, all eyes, all light and all source of everything Good."

[153] *Adv. haer.* II, 1.1 (German: loc. cit., p. 21).

[154] *Adv. haer.* IV, 20.1.

[155] Cf. C. Andresen, „Die Anfänge christlicher Lehrentwicklung," in: the same ed., *Handbuch der Dogmen- und Theologiegeschichte*, Vol. 1 (Göttingen, 1982), pp. 97, 98.

[156] *Grundriß der Dogmengeschichte*, Vol. 1: *Gott und die Welt (Grundrisse 2)* (Darmstadt, 1982), p. 179.

[157] Norbert Brox has made a mistake in his otherwise excellent translation. He translates the final sentence of *Adv. haer.* II, 30.9 (loc. cit., p. 267) as follows: „Since the Son always exists with the Father, he reveals the Father *always and since the beginning* to the angels, archangels, powers and forces and to all those to whom God wants to be revealed" (emphasis added). Here the impression could arise of an eternal revelation function („always"); the Latin version, however, reads as follows: „olim et ab initio semper," that is, the Son revealed „*once and since the beginning* always." The revelation thus occurs *in time* („once") and began with the beginning; it is not at all an eternal, i.e. inner-godly, but an economic function of the Son.

[158] Adolf von Harnack, *Lehrbuch der Dogmengeschichte*. Volume One: *Die Entstehung des kirchlichen Dogmas* (Unaltered photographic reproduction of the 4th edition [Tübingen, 1909]), (Darmstadt, 1964), p. 584.

mediating entities. But *Irenaeus* above all is soteriologically shaped by the Hellenistic nostalgia for deification and that is why he is interested in the incarnation of the Son and the deification that it makes possible for us, as well as – later – in the recapitulation of salvation history, the Story of the Life and Sufferings of Christ: „And if man were not linked with God, then he would have been able to attain no part of immortality. ... Namely, for this purpose is the Word of God become a man and the Son of God a Son of Man, so that man can take up the Word into himself and, adopted, become the Son of God."[159]

Irenaeus must therefore for soteriological reasons insist upon an *independent function* of the Logos in the Creation and, more importantly for him, in revelation, Incarnation and recapitulation – as well as of the Spirit, and along with the entire Hellenistic mentality he is convinced that God himself cannot affect his simplicity through his own activities; to do so He needs Logos and Spirit. These are, however, unlike the emanations of the Gnostics, which in contradiction to God create and redeem in a certain independence, „hands of God"[160] – here he takes up one of *Philo*'s images[161] – and his instruments,[162] so that *through them He himself* is the creator and redeemer: „There is on the other hand only one God, the creator, who is above all sovereignty, power, dominion and force. ... He is the Father, God, creator, finisher and foreman, who, through himself, that is, through his Word and through his wisdom, has made the heaven, earth, seas and everything that is in Him. . . . Through His Word, which is his Son, through him is He revealed and made known to all. ..."[163]

Logos and Spirit are therefore one with God and are before the „beginning" indistinguishable from Him; only afterwards do they make their appearance – the usual scheme since *Philo* and *John 1* – in an independent function and „form." *The Trinity is thus understood entirely in economic and subordinationist terms* – Son and Spirit are lesser forms of the divine being – and as a matter of salvation history, whereas „God Himself" remains one and unseparated. *Irenaeus*, so to speak, moves the Trinity „outwards," outside of God Himself. There, however, in the economy, *Irenaeus* „needs" these hypostases; for the Creation and – even more so – for revelation and the Incarnation, as well as for the work in the Church, Son and Spirit are indispensable because God Himself cannot work directly, but only by means of his „hands."

However, in salvation history, and only there, Son and Spirit do nevertheless obtain the divine characteristic[164]; in the *Epideixis Irenaeus* writes: „Thus is the

---

[159] *Adv. haer.* III, 18.6 (German: TzT 4.1, No. 61).
[160] Cf. *adv. haer.* IV, 20.1.
[161] Cf. pp. 27-29 above.
[162] Cf. *adv. haer.* II, 3.2.
[163] *Adv. haer.* II, 30.9 (German: loc. cit., p. 265).
[164] Thus also F. Courth, *Trinität in der Schrift und Patristik* (Freiburg, Basel, Wien, 1980), p. 70.

Father Lord and the Son Lord and the Father God and the Son God, for that born of God is God. And there is thereby according to His being and according to the strength of His nature one (single) God to acknowledge, but according to the salvation order of our redemption He is quite properly Son as well as Father."[165]

Here it is also still noticeable that the weight of the argumentation is binitarian; in other passages, however, the Spirit is included. What does become clear, though, is the coexistence of monarchianism for God Himself and a binitarian or Trinitarian conception of an economic sort. It remains unclear how full divine being can be declared of Son and Spirit even though their special being is a part only of the domain of the economy.

The doctrine of God put forward by *Clement* of Alexandria († c. 215) is similar to that of *Irenaeus*, although its points of emphasis are different – *Clement* has more recourse to Gnostic motifs – and its formulation is less evolved. For him as well – so to speak – „God as such" is one and simple: „Also one cannot speak of parts in God; for indivisible is the One and therefore also infinite ... and accordingly formless and nameless."[166] In this it is not His Biblical personality, but the Greek-cosmic dimension of God that is placed in the foreground: He is in the Platonic sense „One ... or the Good or Spirit"; he is „the Invisible and Ineffable," the ‚abyss'" that – anti-Gnostically – „has embraced the universe and at the same time taken it up into his bosom."[167]

Out of this „One" goes the Word of God,[168] which he too – motivated by early Jewish angelology – calls an „angel,"[169] and there is also „*the* Third One," the Holy Spirit.[170] *Clement* is – like „the apologists and Philo ... a theologian of the Logos."[171] The emphasis is placed on this Logos, which is „the divine reason of the world personified in Christ"[172] and „is made visible and revealed by the god" and which has appeared in Jesus[173]; as the law of the world the Logos is here – anti-Gnostically – in harmony with the Father.[174] *Clement* considers that the foundations of his economic-Trinitarian concept are already laid in *Plato*'s *Timaeus*, which he believes was „influenced by the Hebraic writings."[175] Thus *Clement*, too, combines an immanently „monarchian" concept of God with an economic doctrine of the Trinity.

---

[165] *Epideixis* 47 (German: loc. cit., pp. 65-6).
[166] *Strom.* V, 12 (German: TzT 2.1, No. 87).
[167] Ibid. (German: ibid.).
[168] *Strom.* V, 12 (German: TzT 2.1, No. 87).
[169] *Pedagogus* I, 58.1, cf. pp. 46 above.
[170] *Strom.* V, 14 (German: TzT 2.1, No. 87).
[171] K. Beyschlag, *Grundriß der Dogmengeschichte*, Vol. 1, loc. cit., p. 195.
[172] K. Beyschlag, ibid.
[173] *Pedagogus* I, 57.1 (German: TzT 4.1, No. 79).
[174] K. Beyschlag, loc. cit., p. 195.
[175] *Strom.* V, 14 (German: TzT 2.1, No. 87).

Tertullian, who was the first to introduce the term *trinitas* in Latin theology,[176] advocates a quite similar doctrine of God, but reflects upon it more systematically than *Irenaeus* and *Clement*, and puts it in a conceptual nutshell. For him God Himself is radically one and the same; granted, there is the Word (and the Spirit) eternally enclosed within Him: „And the Word was with God, and never is it separated from the Father or an other one than the Father, for I and the Father are one and the same."[177] As in *Philo* and *Justin Martyr*, the Logos is thus viewed as identical with God, in such a way that the latter is conceived of along monarchian lines *before* the „beginning."

Only with the beginning of the economy, with the Creation and the subsequent salvation-historical stages, does a Trinity then unfold itself: „the secret of the economy [oikonomiae sacramentum] ... disposes [disponit] the unity in a trinity [unitatem in trinitatem] in that it determines Father, Son and Spirit as three.[178] And, according to *Tertullian*, it is indeed a question here of *one* substance which differentiates itself in „degree," „form" and „appearance [species] because it is a god from which are derived these degrees, forms and appearances under the names of the Father and the Son and the Holy Spirit."[179] Thus Son and Spirit do not possess the eternal perfection of God: It is only when the Word emerged from God at the Creation that „it made him into the Father in that it emerged from him as the Son"[180]; the separate existence of the Word thus began with the being a son, and only from then on is the eternal God the „Father." Hence, Son and Spirit are subordinated to the Father and, in terms of their being, are inferior to the „god as such": „The Father is namely the entire substance [tota substantia], but the Son a derivation of the whole and a part [derivatio totius et portio]. ... Thus as a result the Father is an other than the Son since He is greater than the Son. ..."[181]

Tertullian characterizes Father, Son and Spirit in their separateness with a term which he is the first to introduce into Latin theology: they are three *personae*. The more exact meaning of the concept of person[182] in *Tertullian* is disputed; it is probably to be understood in the sense of the „role" either assumed by a lawyer „in persona" of an affected party in a trial or by an actor. On no account does it have the meaning, first encountered after *Boethius*, of subjectivity, and therefore should not be conceived of in the sense of the

---

[176] *Adversus Praxean* II, 4.

[177] *Adv. Prax.* VIII, 1 (German: TzT 2.1, No. 90).

[178] *Adv. Prax.* II, 4 (German: TzT 2.1, No. 88).

[179] Ibid. (German: ibid.).

[180] *Adv. Prax.* VII, 1 (German: TzT 2.1, No. 89).

[181] *Adv. Prax.* IX, 2 (German: TzT 2.1, No. 91).

[182] A brief summary of the state of research on the etymological, and the philosophical- and theological-historical origins of the term *persona* is provided by *Aloys Grillmeier, Jesus Christus im Glauben der Kirche*, Vol. 1: *Von der Apostolischen Zeit bis zum Konzil von Chalkedon (441)* (Freiburg, Basel, Wien, 1979), pp. 250-252.

modern understanding of person.[183] Thus *persona* is an all-embracing designation of the three economic functions that the Father, Son and Spirit perform[184]: „Hence, whatever the substance of the word has been, I am calling that person and making use of the name of the Son for it and defending ... this as being the second from the Father."[185]

Tertullian thus reflects what until then had functioned as the motivation behind the attempts to think Jewish and Jewish-Christian monotheism together with the Greek god: That this second (and third) god is necessary because the – Greek – god can himself not act and therefore needs lesser divine mediating hypostases for the purpose of constituting the world, conducting history, and, additionally in Christianity, for the purpose of the Incarnation in Jesus and the sanctification. The doubling or the tripling thus has economic (from a modern perspective: cultural soteriological) causes and is thus quite consciously allotted to the domain of salvation history, whereas God – viewed for Himself – remains monarchian: „Therefore, on the one hand, the Trinity [trinitas], which comes from the Father through a series of linked stages [gradus], is in no way an obstacle to the monarchy and, on the other hand, it protects the status of the economy."[186] The Trinity is a reality which is linked up with a beginning in time and which, according to *Tertullian*, even passes in the end: Christ „hands over ... the kingdom to the Father and is again received into the Father," an „eschatological self-supersession of the Trinity."[187]

Less reflected than this is the binitarian view of *Hippolytus* of Rome († 235), who to a certain extent once again repeats the conception of the apologists: The Logos is engendered by the Father „as an inward reflection upon the universe." Separate from the Father, it first existed in the „moment of the emergence from the Begetter, as the first begotten sound." At the command of the Father, it became the ground of the universe and created everything to the satisfaction of the Father.[188]

4.5 From the Economic to the Eternal Trinity

Origen took a decisive step in the development of the doctrine of the Trinity, one which had not yet been so clearly carried out before him. Where this doctrine was previously – in accordance with the motives for its having been

---

[183] Cf. by the present author, *Fundamentalchristologie*, loc. cit., p. 294.

[184] Comparably, the „una persona" in Jesus Christ is to be understood in the sense of the common role in which divinity and humanity collaborate in it (*adv. Prax.* XXVII, 11; cf. by the present author, *Fundamentalchristologie*, loc. cit., pp. 193-4).

[185] *Adv. Prax.* VII, 9 (German: TzT 2.1, No. 89).

[186] *Adv. Prax.* VIII, 7 (German: TzT 2.1, No. 90).

[187] Alfred Adam, *Lehrbuch der Dogmengeschichte*, Vol. 1: *Die Zeit der Alten Kirche* (Gütersloh, ¹1970), p. 167.

[188] *Elenchos* X, 33 (German: TzT 4.1, No. 70).

created – a matter of salvation history, so that, for better or for worse, it remained compatible with the fundamental monotheism or monarchianism, it was now *shifted into God Himself: the economic becomes a God-immanent subordinationism*; the unity of „God Himself" is from now on threatened.

The starting point in the considerations of *Origen* was the question to what extent the Logos and the Spirit could really be God if they had had a beginning in time or to what extent an economic action could be predicated of God which is not – like Himself – eternal. Thus he concluded: „How can one further think or believe that God the Father has ever existed, even just for the slightest instant, without the procreation of this wisdom. ... Therefore we know that God is constantly Father of His only begotten Son, who is, though born from Him ..., without any beginning."[189] Hence the Father is – how could it be otherwise for God – eternally the Father, and as a result the Logos is eternally the Son. The procreation is „eternal and everlasting."[190]

Origen, however, can nevertheless not break away from the traditional *economic functions* of the Son and Spirit – the „raison d'être" for their differentiation from „God Himself"; Son and Spirit mediate the Creation and redemption. Now, however, these economic functions must in the same way be „eternal," without a beginning in time. That is why in the Creation there is, according to Origen, *one stage* that, vis-à-vis the concrete beginning of the reality of the world and history, is preexistent, and a *second stage* that is *temporal*.

The preexistent creation is a world of spirits whose creational mediator is the Logos, „whereas the transcendent pneumatic world of angels comes from the Spirit, as the first being created by the Logos."[191] Although Logos and Spirit are mediators from the Father, they are also a part of this preexistent creation.[192] „Deity and creation thus telescope into one another in the preexistent space."[193] The visible world is for its part – a Gnostic motif – the result of a preexistent fall from grace of the created spirits, but is – anti-Gnostically – not understood as being itself bad, but as being a chance to be tested.

Although the step to an immanent conception of the Trinity has been carried out here for the first time, it becomes clear that the legacy of the economic conception is continuing to exert its influence; Logos and Spirit are thought so closely together with their economic functions that the latter share in the transposing of the former into the eternity of God.

As a consequence of this the subordinationism resulting from the economic conception of the Trinity is also retained – and shifted into God Himself. The Father continues to be – or in terms of Neoplatonic tendencies is even more so

---

[189] *De princ.* I, 2.2 (German: TzT 4.1, No. 81).

[190] Ibid. I, 2.4 (German: TzT 2.1, No. 92).

[191] K. Beyschlag, op. cit., p. 206.

[192] Cf. K. Beyschlag, ibid.

[193] K. Beyschlag, ibid., p. 207.

– the God as such „who holds the universe together"[194]; he is being itself[195] or even the super existence.[196] „The Son, who only penetrates to those creatures endowed with reason (works) at a lesser distance than the Father; for he stands in second position after the Father; at an even lesser distance, the Holy Spirit, who only penetrates to the saints. Thus the power of the Father is in this respect greater than that of the Son and of the Holy Spirit; therefore that of the Son, greater than that of the Holy Spirit."[197] Although *Origen* emphasizes that one ought „not to call anything at all in the Trinity greater or smaller," in the next sentence he once again differentiates the specific degrees of effectiveness of Father, Son and Spirit.[198]

To be sure, the argumentation of *Origen* gave expression to something worthy of consideration: The concept of God – properly conceived – cannot be combined with a beginning in time. But the only possible way to avoid these detrimental effects – namely the return to the one God – was not an option open to *Origen*. Even he, the Alexandrian, needed the world-immanent Logos and – Christologically – the doctrine of two natures, and *thus he was only left with the possibility of transposing the Trinity together with the economic grounds for it and its consequences (Creation, redemption in Jesus Christ*[199]*) into God*. Now the economic differentiation was an inner-godly affair, though the Father retained the monarchian associations previously intended for Him. That this – apart from the preexistence of the created spirits – was not perceived as a new, even more egregious, inadequacy can probably only be comprehended against the background of the historical-cultural context of the day; even the simultaneously emerging Neoplatonism of *Plotinus* divided the divine sphere into three hypostases: the *one* (*tò hén*), the spirit (*nous*) and the (world) soul (*psyché*); through the mediation of the lesser hypostases, spirit and *psyché*, the One was able to be the immanent principle of the cosmos and still remain completely simple and super existent.

---

[194] *De princ.* I, 3.5 (German: TzT 2.1, No. 93).
[195] *De princ.* I, 1.6.
[196] *Adv. Cels.* VI, 64.
[197] *De princ.* I, 3.5 (German: TzT 2.1, No. 93).
[198] *De princ.* I, 3.7 (German: TzT 2.1, No. 94).
[199] According to Origen, the – like all human souls – preexistent soul of Jesus had alone decided against the apostasy from God, so that it was already connected with the divine Logos „prehistorically"; in the „second phase" of the Creation – after the becoming-flesh of this soul and hence also of the Logos – only that which had been established before all time was realized in time. Thus Christology – like the Creation – is shifted back into the preexistence.

4.6 A Monotheistic Line

4.6.1 Monarchianism and Modalism

In the pre-Nicene era there were ecclesiastical regions in which Hellenistic thinking – despite all the linguistic borrowings – was still not so deeply internalized that God would not have sufficed to explain the reality of the world and Jesus would have had to have been seen as the incarnated God in order to be accepted as the mediator of salvation. In this context one had no need – aside from God as such – of a Logos as a world-immanent principle and as a second nature of Jesus Christ. The belief in the One God and in the Jesus chosen by Him was thought to express adequately the „subject-matter" of Christianity. Here God was understood as the undifferentiated *one*; He was conceived of in a monarchian way.

Monarchianism (in Greek, „rule by one"), however, had to make allowances for the talk of Logos/Son and Spirit that was widespread in this area and was even by many groups already being advocated in the sense of an economic doctrine of the Trinity. This is why the monarchians had to take up the terms Logos/Son and Spirit and combine them with their own understanding of God. They attempted this by having their supporters teach Logos and Spirit as *dynámeis*, as „powers" of the one God *(dynamistic monarchianism)*.

Others took up a more static conception and spoke of three ways, or *modi*, in which the one God has – as creator, redeemer and saint – revealed himself outwardly. Advocates of this *modalistic monarchianism* or also simply *modalism* (or, after one of its most distinguished representatives, *Sabellianism*) occasionally specified the consequences of this approach: the One God, the Father, is both creator and subject of the redemption; *He* died for us on the Cross *(Patripassianism)*.

What is being expressed in all these variations is the belief in the undifferentiatedly one and single God, the God of Israel and Father of Jesus. But this simple statement had to take into account the talk of Father and Son and this took place in the variable way described and which is expressed in the complicated-sounding terms.

The representatives of this „monotheistic" line were men stemming from regions that were probably not so thoroughly Hellenized.[200] Some of them also disseminated their teachings in Rome where they apparently met with interest

---

[200] For more on the individual representatives of the various versions of monarchianism, compare the standard works on the history of theology; a brief, but informative overview is provided by Karl Baus in „Von der Urgemeinde zur frühchristlichen Großkirche (*Handbuch der Kirchengeschichte*, ed. Hubert Jedin, Vol. 1 [Freiburg, Basel, Wien, ³1965], pp. 291-298.

and approval, even among the local bishops[201] *Zephyrinus* († 217)[202], *Calixtus I* († 222)[203] and *Dionysius* († 268).[204]

In a prominent way, however, monarchianism was indigenous to the area of Syria. The Eastern Syrian *Paul of Samosata* († after 272), who from 260 (?) was the bishop of the Western Syrian cultural center Antioch, rejected a (physical) godhood of Jesus; he maintained that „two gods would be proclaimed if the Son of God were preached as God."[205] Although God created everything through His Logos – here one would have to take into account the prologue to John – but *Paul* conceived of it as the „non-subsisting knowledge" of God, which was His instrument (*órganon*).[206] Thus he taught „that ‚the Son' only designates the man Jesus in whom the wisdom of God came to dwell; that further ‚the Spirit' is nothing else but the grace that God ... has granted."[207]

A synod in Antioch condemned *Paul* and, at the same time, the thesis that the Logos was of the same nature as the Father (*homoousios*) – the later Nicene formula, which was here obviously conceived of in the sense of an identity of Father and Logos, hence in monarchian terms, and for that reason rejected. This condemnation shows that even in Western Syria powerful groups were supporting a Hellenistic doctrine of God and Christology.

4.6.2 The Doctrine of Arius

The theology of *Arius* is unfairly criticized as being the epitome of heresy: in his doctrine of God he is said to advocate an exaggerated subordinationism to the extent that he calls the Logos the noblest creature, but all the same „only" a creature (*ktísma*)[208]; in his Christology he is said to make Jesus into the

---

[201] Cf. p. 84 below.

[202] According to Hippolytus, *Rufutatio omnium haeresium* IX 11, Zephyrinus thought similarly to the modalists, Sabellius and Kleomenes, both of whom were teaching in Rome at the time; cf. especially 11.3.

[203] According to Hippolytus, ref. IX 12.15-19, Calixtus adopted Sabellianist doctrines: „the Father namely is not another, the Son another, but one and the same is the Spirit, ... And the Spirit become flesh in the Virgin is not different than the Father, but one and the same" (ibid. 12.17, from *Refutatio omnium haeresium*, ed. Miroslav Marcovich [*Patristische Texte und Studien*, eds. K. Aland and P. Mühlenberg, Vol. 25], [Berlin, New York, 1986], p. 353).

[204] Cf. Athanasius, *De decretis Nicaenae synodi* 26-27.

[205] From the *Hymenaeus Epistle* 3 (German: TzT 4.1, No. 87); cf. the fragments from the *Synodal Epistle*: the Son of God was not „descended from heaven" (No. 3 [German: TzT 4.1, No. 88]); Mary gave birth to „a man who was like us but better in every connection" because of the „grace (which lay) upon him," (No. 5; German: ibid.).

[206] Ibid. 4 (German: ibid.).

[207] Karl Baus, „Von der Urgemeinde zur frühchristlichen Großkirche," loc. cit., pp. 293-294.

[208] It is absurd to call the coexistence of God and creature (Logos) subordinationism. If on the one hand there is only God, on the other only creature, that is a clear monarchianism.

incarnation of a mythical figure since the Logos, although a preexistent principle of creation, is not divine.

What is being overlooked here is that *Arius* advocated the monarchianism of his native Syria and was unable to acknowledge any other divine hypostasis next to „God as such." It is true that he did – in contrast to his native tradition – admit that there was a preexistent Logos which constituted the world and was incarnated in Jesus; here he appears to have been taking into consideration the desires of his Alexandrian parish, which could not do without the two ideas. This is also why he took up the economic triadic ideas of the 2nd and early 3rd century according to which the Logos entered into existence „in the beginning." However, *Arius* was also probably influenced by the thinking of *Origen* who held that a temporal beginning (*Arius:* „There was a time in which it [the Logos] did not exist"[209]) excluded the attribute divine. Yet, whereas *Origen* drew the logical conclusion from that, that the generation of the Son must be eternal – whereby he transposed it into God Himself – Arius, the monarchian, went the opposite way: The Logos was precisely for this reason not God, but a creature: „The Son did not always exist; for when everything originated out of the nonexistent, and all creaturely and made natures came into being, the Word of God also came into being out of the nonexistent. ..."[210] Nevertheless, the Son since the beginning of his existence makes God into the „Father" and „therefore there is a triad"[211]; it, however, unifies without confusion the infinitely great God with the hypostases foreign to His nature – because creaturely – of the Son and Spirit.[212]

Because as a pastor in Alexandria *Arius* was forced to take up the traditional triadic economic concepts, but viewed them as merely temporal, and thus in the sense of *Origen*'s non-divine hypostatizations, he, following his monarchian origins – unlike *Origen* – could not transpose them into God Himself. God is for him indivisibly one, Son and Spirit are the first and noblest creatures, and the term triad receives a monarchian meaning and does not mean a triadic structure of God Himself.

---

[209] Fragment from *Thalia* (in Athanasius, *Orationes contra Arianos* 1.5; German: TzT 4.1, No. 91).

[210] Fragment from *Thalia* (Athanasius, *or. c. Ar.* 1.5; German: TzT 4.1, No. 91).

[211] „The Blasphemies of Arius" (in Athanasius, *De decretis Nicaenae synodi* 15.3, No. 16 [German: TzT 4.1, No. 90]).

[212] Ibid., Nos. 17-22 (ibid.).

5. The Linguistic Fixing of the Doctrine of the Trinity in the 4th Century

5.1 The Creed of the First Ecumenical Council of Nicaea (325)

The doctrine of *Arius*, which soon became widespread, encountered strong opposition, above all in the strongly Hellenized areas – in particular in Alexandria – which he had hoped to accommodate by acknowledging the Son and Spirit as separate hypostases; the resistance was primarily Christological: in *Arius* the „schema of the exchange," according to which God becomes man to deify us, did not get the attention it deserved; to correspond to this soteriology, Jesus Christ would have to be God in a comprehensive sense.

The Council of Nicaea, convened and dominated by Emperor *Constantine*, led to the condemnation of *Arius*: the son of God is himself God. Likewise rejected, however, was the subordinationist tradition, according to which there are hypostases of varying strengths of being in God. The comprehensive godhood of the Son – the Spirit is only mentioned in passing („and [we believe] in the Holy Spirit") – is described in a series of expressions: he is „only-begotten, that is, from the substance of the Father, God of God, light of light, true God of true God, begotten not made," and there then follows the most important term for the future concept of God: „consubstantial *(homoousios)* with the Father."[213]

Thus the „Son" is now finally placed at the same level in terms of being as God the Father. Admittedly, God's economic functions are retained: „through whom everything comes to be" (cf. John 1.3) and He is „become flesh and man."[214] Yet despite this retention of functions, the „Son" now has such a comprehensive divinity that *the grounds for the heretofore economic conception of the Trinity no longer apply:* Trinitarian thinking had in fact arisen precisely because the one, single and unchanging God could not act „outwardly" in creation and history and therefore needed the „hands," the Son (and Spirit); these *had* to be of a lesser fullness of being because, after all, in their activity they came into contact with change and plurality. But now – after Nicaea – the Logos is conceived of as consubstantial, so that its character no longer corresponded to the requirements of the economy. The way is paved for a later *defunctionalizing* of the second and third hypostases: creation and redemption are then *one* action of the *one* God outwardly – this according to *Augustine*. Then all that is left over are the terms „Son" and „Spirit," which no longer have – as they did when these ideas originated – any determinable or understandable function; since no one is able to say anymore why they are necessary (to a large extent their history has been „forgotten" to this day), they then become the inner-godly mystery.

---

[213] German: TzT 4.1, No. 28.

[214] German: ibid.

What exactly the expression *homoousios* means cannot be determined at first glance; the council uses it, but does not define it. If one reads it on the basis of the later development of the doctrine of the Trinity, it would have to be translated by „identical in nature"; then Father and Son would – in terms of number – have *one* nature (*numerical identity*).

However, as far as this problem is concerned, this way of proceeding does not seem to be legitimate; one must interpret terms as they were commonly used at the time. But then one can determine that as a rule with *homoousios* two natures were being compared which belong to the same genus, but are two in number – just as, for example, father and son among humans (*generic identity*); then the term means as much as „of the same nature."[215]

This suggests the probability that the council participants considered Father and Son to be numerically two beings that, however, in terms of their genus, are in the same way God. Even more, father and son among men also belong „same-naturedly" to the human species, but are completely different from one another in their characteristics – one is older than the other, perhaps larger or smaller, more intelligent or more stupid, and perhaps does not even resemble the other in appearance. All this is not applicable when speaking of God since according to ancient thought God possesses no characteristics in addition to His nature; all „characteristics" are identical with the „nature" of God. That is why the term *homoousios* includes a fully „qualitative" identity.

Nevertheless, however, the creed teaches – with certainty – that there are two (perhaps three) in God, and these two must be capable of being distinguished from one another, at least in that one is the „Father" and therefore Himself – as one said in the theology at the time – unbegotten, whereas the „Son" is begotten „from the Father ..., that is, from the substance of the Father"; *hence one is original, the other derived.* The following descriptions also suggest this difference: the Son is „God *from* God, light *from* light, true God *from* true God." How can these propositions be otherwise understood than that in God the council participants *conceived of two beings alike in everything except originality and derivation*?

This is also suggested by the structure of the symbol: „The symbol is thus, for example, not composed according to the following schema:

---

[215] According to Ignacio de Urbina, *Nizäa und Konstantinopel* (*Geschichte der ökumenischen Konzilien*, eds. Gervais Dumeige and Heinrich Bacht, Vol. I), (Mainz, 1964), p. 94, *homoousios* was already used in Gnostic writing from the 2nd century and penetrated in the 3rd century „into the vocabulary of the theological school of Alexandria," where it was able to achieve a considerable importance; „however, in doing so, the term did not formally include any *numerical* unity of substance for those natures qualifying as *homoousioi*." A very detailed genesis of the term is provided by J.N.D. Kelly, *Altchristliche Glaubensbekenntnisse, Geschichte und Theologie* (trad. from English by K. Dockhorn), (Göttingen, ³1972), pp. 240-251.

```
                        the Almighty Father
I believe in the one God the only-begotten Son
                        the Holy Spirit.
Instead, the schema looks like this:
                    in one God the Father
I believe           in one Lord Jesus Christ
                    in one Holy Spirit."²¹⁶
```

In other words, the Nicene symbol teaches two (or three) deities that are in everything essentially and qualitatively – but not numerically – identical, apart from being Father, Son (and Spirit). Measured against later Trinitarian theology, it is thus by no means orthodox, but in fact ditheistic (or tritheistic).

5.2 The Post-Nicene Development until the Middle of the 4th Century

5.2.1 The Conflict over the Interpretation of homoousios

Without going into the historical course of events or into each variation and school of thought in detail – the reader is invited to refer to the abundant literature on the subject – in what follows only the most important types of interpretation will be identified; it should be noted in the process that often they can only be summarized under a few major headings because the statements made by some of their exponents are not always exact.

(1) *Arius* and his resolute supporters first resisted the term *homoousios* as a matter of principle, also with the fitting argument that it was not Biblical. These *Arians* or Anomoeans (from Greek, *anhomoios* = „unlike": because they taught that Father and Son were not similar) were at first able to gain ground and triumphed at the *Third Synod in Sirmium* in the year 357. A creed was adopted which read as follows: „... But we cannot and should not preach that there are two Gods ... (there) is one God above everything else. ... And everyone knows ... that the Father is greater and the Son is subordinate to the Father, together with all of the things the Father has dominated."²¹⁷ Despite the use of the word „subordinate," there is in fact no (intradivine) subordinationism being taught her because the Son is „dominated" by the Father „with all of the other things," i.e., is a creature. The concept of God is therefore monarchian.

---

²¹⁶ I. de Urbina, loc. cit., p. 84; cf. Kelly, loc. cit., p. 203.

²¹⁷ German: TzT 4.1, No. 93. Cf also as an example *Eudoxius* († 369/370), who was from 357 to 359 the bishop of Antioch, then later of Constantinople. He wrote: „We believe in the only true God and Father, the only *physis* that is unbegotten and fatherless ... and in the one Lord, the Son, who was pious for he held the Father sacred. He is indeed the only-begotten, more powerful than the entire creation after him, but (he is also) the first-born for he is the most excellent and first of all creatures." (German: TzT 4.1, No. 94).

(2) By far the largest group of theologians accepted the Nicene *homoousios*, but understood it in the sense of *similarity* in substance (Greek: *homoiousios* = similar in substance, Latinized: *homoeusios*). The Homoiusians, incorrectly called Semiarians as well, probably also represent most exactly the conceptions of the majority of those taking part in the Council of Nicaea; they had in fact combined the – generically viewed – *homoousios* with the difference between paternity and filiation. But because this difference had to be conceived of in God as essential and not accidental, the consubstantiality or sameness in substance has thus already in Nicaea been modified in the direction of a similarity in substance – the Homoiusians merely summed up these connections conceptually.

Within this group as well there were certainly different linguistic – and in part substantive – variations. Thus, for example, the Syrian *Eusebius* of Emesa († 359) employed an Antiochene vocabulary from the dynamistic monarchian tradition and called the Logos the „mind" or „power" of God.[218] The more strongly Hellenistic and subordinationist *Cyril* of Jerusalem († 387) professes his faith in the sole God, „unbegotten, without beginning, without origin, completely unchanging,"[219] and says of the „Son": „he is similar in everything to Him who begot him. ... He is the subsisting wisdom and power of God. ... In nothing does he lack the divine dignity."[220] It is superfluous to add that the Homoiusian doctrine contains a ditheism or a tritheism since it assumes in God two or three hypostases which, though generically consubstantial, are actually only similar to one another.

(3) A third group, wishing to avoid unnecessary controversy, wanted as a result to do without the, after all, non-Biblical talk of an *ousia*, a „substance"; they proposed that one simply say that the Son is similar to the Father. These *Homoeans* (from Greek: *homoíos* = similar, Latinized: *homoeos*) can basically be assigned to the Homoiusian camp.

(4) Just a few theologians interpreted the *homoousios* in a direction that would later prevail: they taught the „one-and-sameness of substance," i.e., the numerical singularity of substance of Father and Son: There is only *one* divine substance.

Above all *Athanasius*, bishop of Alexandria († 373), should be counted as belonging to this group. He rejects the pagan belief „that with the Trinity we too are speaking of many gods. Because we do not introduce ... three principles or three fathers. ... Thus we acknowledge only One Principle; the creative Word, however, possesses, according to our teaching, no other Godhead than that of the sole God. ... For there is One Form of the Godhead, which is also in the Word, and one is God the Father, who exists in Himself, since He is in

---

[218] Cf. fragments 1 and 2 (German: TzT 4.1, No. 94).

[219] *Catecheses* 4.4 (German: TzT 4.1, No. 96).

[220] Ibid. 4, 7 (German: ibid.).

everything, appears in the Son, since he penetrates everything, and in the Spirit, since He is effective in everything through the Word in Him."²²¹

In these remarks it is clear that *Athanasius* also still exhibits remnants of Alexandrian subordinationism *insofar as he does not actually anchor the unity of God in the one substance, but in the „Father."* The latter, however, dynamically represents the one and only substance of God in that He also unfolds Himself into Son and Spirit. God's singularity of substance grounded in the Father is kept up so rigorously by *Athanasius* that the Father is in the end – although through the Logos – the principle of the becoming flesh and of the justification; God, and not so much the Logos, became a man in order for us to become God. These almost modalistic conceptions show the direction being taken whenever the *homoousía* is interpreted in the sense of a numerical unity: toward the defunctionalizing of „Word" and „Spirit."

This line of thought was, for example, very pointedly advocated by one of the Homoousians, *Marcellus* of Ancyra († 374/375), who already in Nicaea „was one of the few who was enthusiastically in favor of the *homoousios*,"²²² and who was suspected of *Sabellianism*. God is an undivided *monas*, and the Logos is in Him and from all eternity identical with Him and then emerges from Him. „In the creation of the world and revelation this force existing in God proves to be" a dynamic energy; „for everything that the Father says or does occurs through the Logos. ... God, insofar as He is effective, is the Logos. ... It is not a question of three different beings; rather the ineffable relationship is to be viewed, so to speak, as an expansion or self-unfolding of the one God."²²³

Plainly, this conception met with a positive resonance in Rome; the Roman bishop could not be persuaded to condemn *Marcellus*.²²⁴ In the Latin West, as a result of the less intensive Hellenization, one was more strongly interested in the one God than in His hypostases, and even in the Christology one emphasized more strongly that *God* became man than to make reference to the „Word."

This attempt to save the Biblical monotheism and at the same time to take into account the economic allocation of functions to Son and Spirit, functions which had in the meantime been transposed into God Himself, was unfortunately not taken up in the later history of theology. Although the interpretation of the Homoousians – *homoousios* as „of one and the same substance" – eventually won out, it was later combined by the Cappadocians²²⁵

---

[221] *Third Discourse Against the Arians* 15 (German: TzT 2.1, No. 97).

[222] Adolf von Harnack, *Lehrbuch der Dogmengeschichte*, Volume 2: *Die Entwicklung des kirchlichen Dogmas I* (unrevised photographic reproduction of the 4th edition [Tübingen, 1909]), (Darmstadt, 1964), p. 242, n. 1.

[223] Reinhold Seeberg, *Lehrbuch der Dogmengeschichte*, Volume 2: *Die Dogmenbildung in der alten Kirche* (unrevised photographic reproduction of the 3rd edition [Leipzig, 1923]), (Darmstadt, ⁶1965), p. 97.

[224] Cf. R. Seeberg, ibid., pp. 242.244.

[225] Cf. below 5.3.

in a very contestable way with the concerns of the Homoiusians and became in this form the language of the Trinitarian orthodoxy.

5.2.2 The Transition from a Doctrine of the Binity to the Doctrine of the Trinity

Because with the baptismal formula and other triadic listings the Spirit had in the meantime become a part of the tradition, it was usually mentioned in passing in the previous discussion, though often only in a way that was still practiced by the Council of Nicaea: „And (we believe) in the Holy Spirit." Up to this point the real controversies were concerned with the role, function and dignity of the Logos/Son.

5.2.2.1 The Challenge to the Divinity of the Spirit

After Nicaea, however, a change starts to develop here: Some theologians challenged the godhood of the Spirit. They were soon called *Pneumatomachians* (Greek: *pneuma* = spirit, *macheisthai* = to fight) or – after one of their (perhaps falsely so identified)[226] representatives, *Macedonius* of Constantinople († before 364) – also *Macedonians*.[227] For the most part they acknowledged the divinity of the Son, but with reference to the Biblical texts wanted to limit the Spirit to a serving function and thus to its creatureliness. Their writings are no longer extant; some of their theses are only known from the polemics of their opponents.

5.2.2.2 The Acceptance of the Divine Status of the Spirit

Theological attention was first focused upon the Spirit when its divinity was disputed, as *Basil* of Caesarea († 379) observes: „But (in Nicaea, K.-H. O.) the Holy Spirit was only discussed in passing, without any further elaboration. At the time this question had not yet been raised. ..."[228] After the Logos had been defined as consubstantial with the Father, this also had to have an impact on the Spirit, which until then had not been the subject of a more exact reflection; under these preconditions the triadic formula left no other options open: according to *Basil*, „Those who say the Holy Spirit is a creature must be excommunicated."[229] Nevertheless, at no point, which is not easy to

---

[226] Cf. I. Ortiz de Urbina, loc. cit., pp. 174-175.

[227] The three most important representatives of this line of thought were Eustathius of Sebaste, Eleusius of Cyzicus and Marathonius of Nicomedia.

[228] *Ep.* 125, 3 (German: BKV 46 [Munich, 1925], p. 147).

[229] *Ep.* 125, 3 (German: BKV 46, loc. cit., p. 148).

understand, does he purely and simply name the Spirit with the conceptual terms of God or *homoousios*: „His friends and fellow theologians had already tried to answer this question, first Athanasius of Alexandria, then also Gregory Nazianzen."[230] Still, through *Basil*'s theology a development was set in motion *to understand the Christian conception of God also in the conceptual terms of the Trinity.*

Yet, though a creatureliness of the Spirit came increasingly to be rejected, the Spirit's inclusion within God still remained difficult. In what relationship does the Spirit stand to Father and Son? Is the Spirit subordinate to them or of equal rank? These questions were primarily taken up and resolved for the future by *Basil* of Caesarea. His commitment to the subject has a biographical background: He is fascinated by the monasticism which is spreading everywhere and which he is organizing cenobitically in Cappadocia by giving it a „rule" (the „Rule of St. Basil the Great"); with this rule he wants to orient monastic life along the lines of the early Christian community in Jerusalem.

The Spirit played a role both in the early Christian community, which after all understood itself – in possession of the Spirit – as a community of the last days, and in the sprituality of monasticism, in the latter case – in the struggle against the demons and in the constantly renewed attempt to live spiritually – as a nearly tangible, perceivable quantity. This existential and spiritual basis seems to motivate *Basil* to battle for the establishment of the Spirit's place in theology as well.

Another factor is also involved: as a young man *Basil* had let himself be baptized; the baptism with its triadic formula represented for him a vivid experience of initiation. In a letter he writes: „In accordance with this baptism we profess our faith, and the profession of faith corresponds to our doxology in that together with the Father and the Son we extol the Holy Spirit because we are convinced that it does not stand outside the divine nature."[231]

Basil's anthropology also plays an important role: For him man is the *image* (*eikón*) of God (cf. Gen. 1.26). However, the Biblical testimony is understood by him – as was usually the case in the early Christian era – in the sense of a „natural" affinity; man is in his – especially spiritual – nature God's image and is organized upon that basis. He can therefore only properly realize himself if he *imitates God* (*mímesis theou*), that is, if he lives spiritually – „in the prevention of the evil passions."[232] As in monasticism in general, for him it is less a question of following in the (historical) footsteps of *Jesus* than of living the – Hellenistic – pneumatic life, in which one strives for an approximation with God. But because this is our goal, the Spirit that guides us in the process must itself be divine; it is, after all, supposed to „deify" us.

---

[230] H.J. Sieben, „Introduction," in Basilius, *De spiritu sancto. Über den heiligen Geist*, trans. and introd. H.-H. Sieben, Fontes Christiani, Vol. 12 (Freiburg, Basel, Vienna, Barcelona, Rome, New York, 1993), p. 43; cf. ibid. pp. 42-50 for the discussion of this question.

[231] *Ep.* 159, 2 (German: BKV 46, loc. cit., p. 175).

[232] Basil, *De spiritu sancto* 9, 23 (German: Fontes Christiani, Vol. 12, loc. cit., p. 141).

Basil goes so far – for the first time in the history of theology – as to link the Hellenistic principle of baptism (God or the Logos becomes a man so that we may become divine) not with the incarnation of the Logos, but with the Spirit: „Verily, through the Spirit the hearts are exalted. ... By enlightening those who have been purified of their sins, it makes them through the community with it into men full of spirit. Just as bright and translucent bodies under entering light themselves begin to light up ..., so too do the spirit-bearing souls radiate ... this grace to other people as well. Whence comes ... the infinite joy, the abiding in God, *the approximation with God and the highest of all striving: to become God oneself.*"[233] In other words, *the schema previously used to establish the godhood of the Logos is now being used to provide security for the divine status of the Spirit.* Here the Spirit becomes the real mediator of our – Hellenistic – salvation. After the Son was elevated by Nicaea to the transcendent height of the Father and can no longer be a „lesser" figure, it is now the Spirit that works among us. But only the *divine* Spirit can hallow us: „The creature serves; the Spirit liberates ... the creature is hallowed, but the Spirit is that which hallows."[234]

From these positions *Basil* engages in the battle for the dignity of the Spirit, refers to its being named in the baptismal order and in the doxology (in the „eulogy"). His opponents object that in the New Testament the Spirit is nowhere doxologically paralleled with the Father and Son; for this reason the same honor ought not be granted to him, much less should he be worshipped. *Basil* – again basing himself here on the baptismal order and on the „holy" that is always used to characterize the Spirit – replies that between the Spirit and the Father and Son there exists a physical community; the doxology is a consequence of the baptismal order.

Other theologians went a step further; increasingly from now on they expressly taught the Spirit's godhood, which they considered themselves to be forced to do above all as a result of the Spirit's traditionally being named at the same time as the Father and Son. „It is also absurd to name and praise together what are by nature dissimilar. For what community or what similarity does the creature have with the Creator?" as *Athanasius* thinks, for example.[235]

Considerations of this sort were immediately plausible against the background of Hellenistic-Christian thinking and the theological situation in the second half of the 4th century, and so it is no surprise that in the creed of the *First Council of Constantinople* in the year 381, which increasingly came to be recognized as ecumenical in the course of the 5th century,[236] without further disputes, several passages on the Spirit were added which underscored his divinity: „And (we

---

[233] Basil, *De spir. sanct.* 9.23 (German: Fontes Christ. 12, loc. cit., pp. 141-143 [italic emphasis, K-H- O.]).

[234] Basil, *Ep.* 159, 2 (German: BVK 46, loc. cit., p. 175).

[235] *First Epistle to Serapion of Thmuis* 9 (written between 358 and 362; German: TzT 2.1, No. 98).

[236] Cf. 5.4 below.

believe) in the Holy Spirit, the Lord and giver of life, who proceedeth from the Father, who is together honored and exalted with the Father and the Son, who has spoken through the prophets."[237]

The formulations concerning the Spirit give the impression that behind them there stands a theology that is a little older than the level of discussion achieved in the meantime – thus, for example, there is no talk of a *homoousia* of the Spirit. Although the Spirit is indirectly attributed divine „qualities," for instance, being worshipped together with the Father and the Son and his proceeding from the Father. At the time of the council, however, the conceptual reflection was already a step further. In addition, one receives from the „entire style of the creed, its beautiful balance and its easy flow ... more the impression of a piece of liturgy which has evolved naturally in the life and church service of the Christian parish than of an artificial product of a council."[238] It must thus be assumed that the council took over and at most revised the text or was even unaware of it; then it would only have been attributed to it afterwards.[239] Now in any event – as a result of the linking of this symbol with a council which since Chalcedon in 451 had been deemed to be ecumenical – *the divine status of the Spirit and as a result a Trinitarian conception was codified church-wide for the first time.*

5.3 The Formula Orthodoxy

5.3.1 One Substance – Three Hypostases

Basil of Caesarea takes as his starting point the Father, Son and Spirit as well as the one God. In the prior tradition various formal terms were employed for unity and trinity, above all „substance" (*ousía*) and *hypóstasis* (usually used in the sense of substance, hence synonymous with *ousía*), and – in *Basil*'s thinking – they were not always used correctly:

„1. Because many do not recognize in the mysterious doctrines a distinction between *essence* (οὐσία, which is something general, and the term *person* ὑπόστασις[240] and they link the two terms arbitrarily in the belief that it is of no consequence if one says essence or person (hypostasis, K.-H. O.), ... therefore, so that you (the addressee is *Basil*'s brother, *Gregory of Nyssa*; K.-H.

---

[237] German: TzT 4.1, No. 30.

[238] G.N.D. Kelly, loc. cit., p. 322; cf. for more specific details of the origin of the symbol, ibid., pp. 294-339, and I. Ortiz de Urbina, loc. cit., pp. 207-232.

[239] Cf. Kelly, loc. cit., p. 322. The symbol was probably created two to three centuries before the council.

[240] „Person" is in this place and at this time a still inadequate translation of the term *hypóstasis* made on the basis of later Latin conceptions; in English it is better to leave „hypostasis" untranslated.

O.) do not also fall victim to the same error, I have written a treatise on the subject. ...
2. Of all the designations those that are suitable for a series of (numerically) different things have a more general meaning, as for example, the word man. Anyone who pronounces this word is thus speaking of the general nature, but is not designating any (particular, K.-H. O.) man who would be personally identified by this name. Thus, for example, Peter is not more man than Andreas, John or Jacob. ...
3. Therefore what we wish to say is that the word „person" (hypostasis) is meant to designate something individual. ...
4. ... For this reason we say that the observed features of the Trinity, by means of which the propriety (peculiarity, K.-H. O.) of the faith's traditional Persons (hypostases, K.-H. O.) is represented, are in the community of essence incompatible and incommunicable. ... As far as the immeasurableness, inconceivability, as far as the uncreated and unlimited being and all such characteristics are concerned, there is in life-giving nature no difference. ...
5. ... Thus our discussion has viewed something common and something particular in the Trinity: With reference to the essence, the talk is of the common ground; the Person (hypostasis), however, expresses the peculiarity of the individual."[241]

The conceptual schema established by *Basil* of the one essence (*ousía*) or nature (*physis*) and the three hypostases or three *prósopa*[242] is to this day *the formula of Trinitarian orthodoxy*. It made it possible to name the unity and trinity in God in such a way that both the trinity would possesses a reality and the monotheism would – apparently – be preserved; everything that the term God comprises is given numerically only once in the one essence and is at the same time common to all three hypostases.

5.3.2 A Latent Tritheism

Nevertheless, by no means are all the problems solved by this formula, for *Basil* takes the Trinity, and also the separate economic functions of the Father, of the Son, of the Spirit, as the starting point of his argumentation, and he only then asks – in a second step – about the unity. In the comparisons he makes to explain his terms, Father, Son and Spirit appear as different „specimens" of

---

[241] *Ep.* 38 (c. 370, letter to his brother Gregory; German: TzT 4.1, No. 101); cf. Basil, *ep.* 236, 6: Essence and Person (οὐσία καὶ ὑπόστασις) differ from one another just as the general differs from the particular, just as, for example, the living being differs from an individual human being. ..." (German: BKV Vol. 46 [Munich, 1925], p. 294; cf. *ep.* 210, 4: „For the nature of the Father and of the Son and of the Holy Spirit is the same, and *one* is the Godhead" (German: ibid., p. 238).

[242] *Prósopon* literally means „countenance," „face," and was used above all in Syrian theology for the point of unity in Christology.

one species – as is the case for Peter, Andreas or John or in general for individual human beings who belong to the species „man" or „living being." And each of the three hypostases is allotted to a different economic activity; on the creation of the angels *Basil* writes: „Think, in the act that created them, the Father as the first, the Son as the creative, the Spirit as the consummating cause, so that the ‚ministering spirits' (Hebr. 1.14) exist through the will of the Father, come into being through the essence of the Son, are consummated through the assistance of the Spirit."[243]

This is why Father, Son and Spirit do in fact each possess a specific reality: „one must acknowledge that each Person (*hypostasis*, K.-H. O.) exists as a real hypostasis"[244]; otherwise there is the danger of lapsing „into Judaism," just as „that anyone who does not acknowledge the common ground of the essence falls victim to polytheism."[245] It is clear that the unity of the essence is being taught here; it is, however, just as obvious that there is granted to each element of the trinity a separate existence, which cannot prevent a tritheism from being given within the common essence.

In his differentiation of *ousía* and *hypóstasis*, which to a great extent were used synonymously in the Greek philosophical tradition, *Basil* is following the example of Neoplatonic discursive practices which identify a certain distinction between the two terms: *ousía* is there the – entirely general – essence; *hypóstasis* could have the meaning of a – more concrete – „realization" of the essence or its – concrete – execution. In this sense *Basil* comprehends the three hypostases as three different „concrete" realizations of the one Godhood. What would remain to be asked here is whether the divine essence which concretely hypostatizes itself threefold is really being understood in the sense of a numerical identity; in any event, *Basil* also speaks of a „community of essence" and „community of nature."[246] *Leo Scheffczyk* observes with regard to the three Cappadocians: „To this extent it is in fact true that the Cappadocians interpreted the ὁμοούσιος (*homoousios*, K.-H. O.) in the sense of the ὁμοῖος κατ' οὐσίαν (similar in essence, K.-H. O.) and thus executed the building of a bridge to the Homoiusians. ..."[247]

How little monotheism is ensured by the concept of the one essence is demonstrated by *Basil*'s attempt to anchor the unity of God – as in the subordinationist tradition – in the „Father" rather than in the „essence" of God; his concept of the unity of the three hypostases looks like this: ἐκ (from), διά (through), ἐν (in).[248] There is a monarchy of the Father, *from* whom everything derives *through* the Son and results *in* the Spirit: „For in fact there

---

[243] *De spiritu sancto* 38 (ch. 16); German: Fontes Christiani, Vol. 12, loc. cit., pp. 185-187.
[244] *Ep.* 210, 5 (German: BKV Vol. 46, loc. cit., p. 240).
[245] Ibid. (German: ibid.).
[246] *Ep.* 38, 4 (German: TzT 4.1, No. 101).
[247] „Lehramtliche Formulierungen und Dogmengeschichte der Trinität," loc. cit., p. 179.
[248] Cf. *De spir. sanct.* 8 (ch. 5).

is only one single origin for all beings, which creates *through* the Son and is consummated *in* the Holy Spirit."[249]

5.3.3 A Stronger Emphasis on the Unity of God with a Residual „Tritheism"

Both of the other Cappadocians, *Gregory Nazianzen* and *Gregory of Nyssa*, held to the course proposed by *Basil*. *Gregory* Nazianzen underscored the *homoousia* of God[250] and: „For us there is only one God, since there is only one Godhead."[251] In his case the numerical self-sameness of God is clearer than in the case of his friend *Basil*; but just like the latter he grounds the unity of God with subordinationist language in the monarchy of the Father: „If we also believe in three, they are still traced back to that one from whom they originated."[252]

Thus *Gregory* can also not avoid the threat of an inner-godly tritheism; although he wants to avoid all the images for God that are taken „from earthly things" – that would be „sheer madness"[253] – he then nevertheless compares the indivisibility of God „in the different ones" with „three suns united with each other," which have only *one* „mixture of light," and speaks of the „three that we worship,"[254] and – in the plural – of „realities."[255] Beyond that, he wards off the attempt to see in God only a single hypostasis, since then „all that will be left over in the profession of faith in the one Father and Son and Holy Spirit will be empty names,"[256] and under no circumstances does he want that.

Of *Gregory* of Nyssa *H. Vorgrimler* thinks that he takes as a starting point the infinity of God's essence and „thus also in Trinitarian fashion the unity of the essence, not the trinity."[257] That may occasionally appear so, and his theology certainly revolves more emphatically around the unity of God; nevertheless, he speaks so pointedly of the independent reality of the hypostases that he is in fact propagating a tritheism. He ascribes „simplicity" to the Logos. If one acknowledges that, „one must also admit that the Word is independent life, not just participating in life. Now if the Word is alive, because it is itself life, it also possesses will power; for there is nothing living which would be without

---

[249] *De spiritu sancto* 37 (ch. 16); German: Fontes Christiani, Vol. 12, loc. cit., p. 187.
[250] *Oratio* 31, 10 (Fifth Theological Discourse [380]).
[251] Ibid. (German: TzT 2.1, No. 105).
[252] Ibid. (German: ibid.).
[253] Ibid. Or. 31.10 (German: TzT 2.1, No. 104).
[254] Ibid. 31.14 (German: TzT 2.1, No. 105).
[255] *Or.* 31, 10 (German: ibid., No. 104).
[256] *Or.* 20, 6 (German: TzT 4.1, No. 103).
[257] Introduction to Gregory of Nyssa, in TzT 2.1, No. 106 (p. 120).

will. The reverence for God, however, demands the further conclusion that this will be powerful."[258]

However, what else does that mean but that the Logos is a subject subsisting for itself? And it is this very point that *Gregory* develops in the following: „... likewise the Word of God is by its independent being different from that from which it has this independent being; but because it shows in itself what we know in God, it is in its nature identical with Him in whom the same characteristic qualities are found."[259] All of the talk of the unity appears to lead no further than to understand it *generically*, and it is also otherwise impossible when one speaks of three independent realities. Even if numerically *one* essence were assumed, according to *Gregory* the three hypostases *in it* would have to possess „independent being."

5.3.4 The Etymological Doctrine of the Trinity

As already explained, *Basil* still – as in the tradition before him – allots separate economic functions to the three hypostases although this actually should now have been unthinkable given the prerequisite of *one* divine essence. But the unity had not yet been so radically imagined, and even the other two Cappadocians show deficits in this area – in spite of their efforts to place a stronger emphasis on the unity.

Nevertheless, with the talk of the one God and of His one essence, the attention had turned from the economic activity to the divine sphere itself, and in time it became necessary to establish the trinity above all and soon exclusively on an inner-trinitarian basis, since after all it has existed *from all eternity* – and not just since the „beginning," that is, since the beginning of the economy. Here it is a question of *a new task*, given the fact that the doctrine of the Trinity had in its origins until then been established on an economic – on an exclusively economic – basis, and had until then been so understood and conceived of by the theologians: it had proven itself to be the hypostatization of the action of God outwards.

What remains, however, if the recourse to this action in its appropriation to the individual hypostases becomes increasingly problematic because the Trinity is conceived of as an eternal quantity? Then all that is left are the terms *Father, Son and Spirit* and a few other expressions commonly used since the time of the New Testament, such as the Logos – the Word – or the speaking of the Son as „the image of the invisible God" (Col. 1.15).

Basil consistently falls back on such words when he wants to explain the hypostatic peculiarities. Proper to the Son is precisely, as the *term* says, the being born or begotten, to the Father, the begetting and – for Himself – the lack of any kind of derivation: Nobody would attribute „either birth to the

---

[258] *Oratio catechetica magna*, Large Catechesis 1.1 (German: TzT 4.1, No. 105).

[259] Ibid. 1, 3 (German: ibid.).

Father or not being born to the Son"[260]; and anyone who speaks of the Son in doing so necessarily also thinks of the Father, and in the Son one can see the copy of the original, except for the „unborn nature of the Father."[261] Even the term Spirit (Greek: *pneúma*, from *pnéo* = to breathe) served *Basil* to paraphrase its inner-godly peculiarity: It is „not like the Son begotten, but ... the breath of His (the Father's, K.-H. O.) mouth. By ‚mouth' no part of the human body is meant, and by ‚breath' no breathing that passes away. ‚Mouth' is rather to be thought in a manner fitting to God and ‚breath' as the living being that rules over sanctification."[262] Here it is interesting that there is even talk of an essence (*ousía*) of the Spirit, where it should actually be called *hypóstasis*.

In the years to come, the more the unity of God is placed into the foreground and hence the economy of salvation tends to become problematic or even useless – explicitly in *Augustine*, who regards more than one action of God externally as unthinkable[263] – in the description of the hypostatic peculiarities, the less there remains of anything with which one can describe – in an inner-Trinitarian way – Father, Son and Spirit in their diversity.

What is left are their names or other symbolic terms from the Bible. These are now enlisted in order to be able to express who or what they are. Even *Gregory Nazianzen* interprets the meaning of Father, Son and Spirit etymologically: „the Father (is) the one without beginning, the Son is the one begotten without beginning, the Holy Spirit is the one proceeded or proceeding without begetting,"[264] or he speaks of „being unbegotten, being begotten and proceeding"[265] as the hypostatic peculiarities.

Gregory of Nyssa even justifies the (generic) *homoousia* of the Logos with the words father and son: „no reasonable person will say that a master builder has begotten a house, but with the names father and son it is declared that by nature both belong together ..." and „the Son is consubstantial with the Father"[266]; much the same is true for the term „word": „as soon as one says ‚word,' one must also think of the father of the word ..., because there is no word without its stemming from someone."[267] Even the hypostatic particularity of the Spirit is explained, as in *Basil*, on the basis of the term itself: „The Holy Spirit is to

---

[260] *Ep.* 38, 7 (German: TzT 2.1, No. 102).

[261] Ibid. 38, 8 (German: ibid.).

[262] *De spir. sancto* 46 (ch. 18), German: Fontes Christiani, Vol. 12, loc. cit., pp. 211-213.

[263] Cf. below 6.3.1.

[264] *Or.* 30,18 (German: TzT 2.1, No. 103); the term „to proceed" refers to John 15.26: „the Spirit of truth, which proceedeth from the Father"; cf. *Or.* 20, 7. In John, however, the „proceeding" is related to the economy, whereas in Gregory it is conceived of as an eternal process.

[265] *Or.* 31.9 (German: ibid., No. 104).

[266] *The Lord's Prayer, 3rd Discourse,* V (German: BKV Vol. 56 [Munich, 1927], p. 122).

[267] *Or. catech. magna.*, *Large Catechesis* 1.3 (German: TzT 4.1, No. 105).

be compared to the breath that we expel in speaking."[268] *Gregory* even goes one step further and reflects on *the logical peculiarity* of these statements – concretely, he is referring to the Father and His Word – in saying that here it is a question of *determinations of relationship*, of *relational terms*: „... since furthermore the word is *distinct* from the one who pronounces it – the correlative character of the expression ‚word' is included in the fact that as soon as one says ‚word' one must also think of the father of the word – we thus distinguish the word, I say, because of the just-mentioned correlative character attributed to the word as such, rationally and necessarily, as soon as we hear it, from the one whom it is from. ..."[269]

In this passage hypostatic particularities are for the first time explained by having recourse to the *relational structure* of the designations Father and Word – a, so to speak, *formalized etymology*. Later *Augustine* will refer back to these guidelines and develop his conception of the Trinity with the help of this understanding of relationship.[270] What looks so clever and complicated thus has quite simple grounds: If the Trinity must be explained while leaving aside the economic functions that were decisive for its being created, *the only thing left are the names which structurally bear within themselves indications of their relationship*; the Trinity then becomes, because of its emptiness, a mystery that is hard to fathom.

These tendencies are of course only rudimentary in the three Cappadocians since they – contrary to the system – still allow economic aspects to be included in the explanation of the Trinity and thus exhibit, despite the emphasis on the *one* essence, a latent tritheism. But they had pointed out the direction that was going to be taken.

5.4 The New Consensus

The Trinitarian discussions of the day were conducted very passionately in the East. On the situation in Constantinople, *Gregory Nazianzen* writes: „This city is full of artisans and slaves, each of whom is a profound philosopher and preaches in the workshop or on the street. If you want to change a piece of silver for someone, he explains to you how the Father differs from the Son; if you ask for the price of a loaf of bread, you hear that the Son is less than the Father; and if you inquire whether your bath is ready, you receive as an answer that the Son came into existence from nothing. ..."[271] the impassioned participation even of the theological laity in the discussion shows that the

---

[268] Thus Hermann Josef Sieben on Gregory of Nyssa in his introduction to *Basilius*, „Über den Heiligen Geist," in Fontes Christiani Vol. 12, loc. cit., p. 53.

[269] *Or. catech. magna.*, *Large Catechesis* 1, 3 (German: TzT 4.1, No. 105).

[270] Cf. below 6.3.2.

[271] German in Horst Dallmayr, *Die großen vier Konzilien. Nizaea, Konstantinopel, Ephesus, Chalkedon* (München, 1961), p. 108.

questions involved here were existentially important to them. It is, then, all the more surprising that these discussions quickly died down.

As unsatisfactory as the Cappadocians' conception of the Trinity was, it soon gained acceptance in the entire church. Their handy formula seemed finally to clarify the subject matter; in any case it made the Trinitarian language less unwieldy. This was promoted by the symbol, which in Chalcedon in 451 was ascribed to the *First Council of Constantinople* in 381, was viewed as a confirmation of the Cappadocian doctrine and which increasingly made its way into the liturgy as the *Nicene-Constantinople Creed*. As *Leo Scheffczyk* observes: „For the East the even more sweeping claim was made that, with this symbol and the theology of the Cappadocians underlying it, the theological unfolding and fathoming of the mystery of the Trinity had also been essentially completed, even though John of Damascus was also to perform an instructive systematization."[272]

One would probably have to consider that the reason for the quick calming of the Trinitarian discussion was that everything that one could say on this topic with the available Hellenistic-Christian linguistic means had been said; an increase in the unity of God would have deprived the soteriologically indispensable trinity of its reality, a stronger emphasizing of the trinity would have fully abolished the monotheism. *The Cappadocian formula had attained the limits of what could be formulated.*

For this reason *Scheffczyk*'s notion concerning the completion of the Trinity discussion in the East is correct; there are no longer any major changes beyond the Cappadocians and this form of the doctrine of the Trinity has shaped the theology of the Eastern Orthodox churches to this day. With it, however, it seems that a certain trend can be made out towards even more of an emphasis on the number „three" to the disadvantage of the unity.

Above all in connection with the Christological discussion, an attempt was made to reconcile the aporetic side-by-side juxtaposition of the two natures by seeking a point of unity which, though not natural – that being no longer possible after Chalcedon – would nevertheless possess a certain fullness in terms of content: *Monenergetism* presumed *one enérgeia* (a principle of activity), that of the Logos, in Jesus Christ; *Monotheletism* one will, that of the Logos. Obviously one was ascribing to the Logos an *energeia* and a will of its own. Thus the *Second Council of Constantinople* in the year 553, the fifth of the so-called ecumenical councils, already formulated that „one out of the Trinity"[273] became a man; in this phrase the Logos appears as something like a subject, and the Incarnation can only be appropriated to him. The passage cited is repeated by the *Third Council of Constantinople* in the year 680/81, the so-called Trullan Synod and sixth „ecumenical council," despite its condemnation of Monenergetism and Monotheletism. The doctrine of the *anhypostasia* of the human nature – it does not have a hypostasis, a „personality" of its own – and

---

[272] „Lehramtliche Formulierungen und Dogmengeschichte der Trinität," loc. cit., p. 182.
[273] *Heis täs hagías triádos* (German: TzT 4.1, No. 35).

of its *enhypostasia* in the divine Logos – only by uniting with the Logos does Jesus Christ „hypostatize" in the Logos – likewise supports the idea of the subject-like nature of the Logos; at any rate this was conceived of in such a way that it would have to come into conflict with a human „person" of Jesus.[274] *Luise Abramowski* accurately characterizes this consensus: „To be sure, inherent in the ultimately achieved neo-Nicene solution is the problem of the danger of a tritheistic doctrine if one understands the three hypostases only as three copies of the one divine οὐσία."[275]

---

[274] Cf. by the present author, *Fundamentalchristologie*, loc. cit., pp. 292-302.
[275] „Zur Trinitätslehre des Thomas von Aquin," loc. cit., p. 472.

6. The Trinitarian Development in the Latin West

6.1 Trinitarian Disinterest

The previous overview may have already made it clear that the Latin West did not play a major role in the development of the doctrine of the Trinity up until the First Council of Constantinople. It participated only marginally in the discussions and was itself not excited by them; its soteriological hopes and fears were concentrated upon other problems.[276] That is also the reason it was occasionally able to intervene in a moderating and mediating way in the violent Eastern controversies; aside from the Greek-speaking *Irenaeus* or *Hippolytus*, scarcely any of the theologians in the West understood why „the Greeks" were so passionately involved in them. When from time to time the West did exert an influence, then its tendency was usually to preserve the unity of God. „God" was more important for the West than Father, Son and Spirit. The need to hypostatize the economic functions of God was here only seldom felt.

In the West the Incarnation idea taken over from the Eastern discussion was also attached less to a separate Logos (*verbum*) than to God Himself. The expression „God became man" was more important than „the *verbum* became man"; whereas in the East the *logos-sarx* schema was widespread, the West preferred the *deus-homo* pattern, like the Antiochenes, but for different reasons. It thus had no soteriological interest worth mentioning in a mediation of the „holy exchange" between the infinite and the finite by means of a divine intermediary figure, the Logos. Here man stood directly facing God, and this relationship was focused not on the longing for „existential" deification, but in the redemption from sin[277]; thus, according to the Latin version of the principle of exchange: „Christ is therefore ... come into sin, as we (through him, K.-H. O.) are come into righteousness."[278]

Admittedly, the Eastern dogmas possessed authority and were obediently accepted; as far as that goes, in the West the Incarnation was also ascribed to the *verbum*. But then usually a few sentences further on in a work by the same theologian one once again encounters talk of the *deus incarnatus*, of God-become-man.

Of course, here, as always, there are exceptions. Thus, for example, the North African *Lactantius* († after 317) advocates a view of the Logos strongly influenced by angelology. However, he is atypical insofar as he had acquired Gnostic and Platonic ideas during a stay in Asia Minor. Be that as it may, he –

---

[276] Cf. by the present author, *Fundamentalchristologie*, loc. cit., pp. 147-150.

[277] Cf. by the present author, *Fundamentalchristologie*, loc. cit., pp. 343-362.

[278] Augustine, *Enchir. ad Laurentium sive de fide et spe et caritate* 13, 41 (c. 423, German: TzT 4.1, No. 149); cf M. Luther, Brief an Georg Spenlein (1516): „You, Lord Jesus, are my righteousness, I however am your sin ... you have taken on that which you were not, and you have given me that which I was not" (German: TzT 4.2, No. 200).

like the apologists – ascribes the Incarnation to the Logos; however – Gnostically – the second hypostasis that proceeds from God, the second „spirit," is an evil being or the Devil.[279]

The basic tendency of placing the unity of God in the foreground can be illustrated by a number of examples: *Irenaeus* and *Tertullian* both take up *Justin Martyr*'s doctrine of the Logos, but also want the hypostatic unfolding to be limited to the economy and stick to a monarchian idea for God Himself.[280] Even in Rome itself there was, as has been briefly mentioned,[281] a clear trend towards insisting on the unity of God – even including modalistic ideas. The Roman bishop *Zephyrinus* († 217) issued a statement[282] on the Trinitarian disputes, „which was nevertheless not totally free of modalistic influences."[283] His successor *Calixtus I* († 222) also expressed a similar point of view. Although the text of his theses has been lost, his views can be inferred from the polemics of Hippolytus against him.[284] *Hippolytus* claims that *Calixtus* had – because of his doctrine of the Logos – called him a ditheist. *Calixtus* thus probably saw the unity of God as being jeopardized. In a similar fashion the Roman bishop *Dionysius* († 268) pleaded in a letter to his fellow bishop and namesake in Alexandria for the unity of God; in spite of one's speaking of Father, Son and Spirit, the *monas*, God, must not be torn into three: „One after another, I would like first of all to criticize with good cause those who tear apart, dismember and destroy the holiest doctrine of the Church of God, the ‚absolute rule' (of God), into any three powers and any three separate hypostases and deities whatsoever. ... One ... should believe in God the Father, the Absolute Ruler, and in Jesus Christ, His Son, and in the Holy Spirit – but in such a way that the Logos is united with the God of the universe."[285]

After Nicaea the Latinists interpreted the *homoousios* in seeming unanimity in the sense of the numerical self-sameness of essence; in this state of affairs, in turn, the interest in the one God becomes evident, while the three hypostases – except for the designation God the Father – do not seem to fascinate them very much.

---

[279] Cf. *Epitone* 37: „In the beginning, before the foundation of the world, God from the source of his eternity ... begot of himself a Son. ... This latter is the power and the reason of God. ... And of all the angels that God formed out of his breath, he alone has ... been called God. ... On the first and second God, Plato has also ... expressed his views" (German: TzT 4.1, No. 77). In *Div. inst.* II, 8, 7, he says of the second spirit that God produced from Himself that he is the Devil.

[280] Cf. above 4.4.

[281] Cf. above p. 66-67.

[282] Reported by Hippolytus, *ref.* IX, 11, 3.

[283] L. Scheffczyk, loc. cit., p. 175.

[284] *Ref.* IX, 12, 15-19; cf. note 203.

[285] *Letter Against the Sabellians* (between 259-268?), in Athanasius, *Ep. de decret. Nic. Syn.* 26 (German: TzT 4.1, No. 73).

6.2 The Difficulty of the Translation

This is also the reason why the reception of the theology of the Cappadocians – especially their talk of the three hypostases – raised problems. In Latin *hypóstasis* was translated by *substantia*, which, for example, to *Hieronymus* sounded heretical,[286] and for *Augustine* as well a semantic distinction between *ousía* and *hypóstasis* was „heretofore unknown and therefore surprising."[287] He speaks of *one* essence (*essentia*) of God and explains: „In this I am calling essence that which is expressed in Greek by οὐσία. For us the word substance is more commonly used for that: Of course the Greeks also speak of hypostasis. But I do not know how they can claim to differentiate ousia and hypostasis." Some Latin theologians, as *Augustine* reports, adopted the Cappadocian formula: „In Latin it is called one essence and three substances."[288] In fact there was already a new translation of hypostasis by the – not very common but basically with *substantia* synonymous – term *subsistentia* by *Marius Victorinus* († after 362), but *Augustine* had not yet encountered it,[289] even though he had read several of the writings of this Christian-Latin Neoplatonist. He therefore did not know what to do with three hypostases, as *Luise Abramowski* emphasizes: „Augustine would have immediately rejected *tres substantiae* as past endurance for Latin ears. *Boethius* extends his formula to include the customary *tres personae*, but finally reports that the ecclesiastical usus loquendi (linguistic usage, K.-H. O.) excluded three substances in God. We thus see that in the West a hundred years after Augustine there still exists no feeling of confidence in the entire neo-Nicene formula, one οὐσία, three hypostases, three πρόσωπα : Augustine had already suggested that for the one οὐσία it would be better to say *essentia*, and in the West for the three πρόσωπα one had always said three persons (see Tertullian)."
Boethius was admittedly already aware of the talk of three subsistences, but he simply does not propose the hoped-for formula – one essentia, three subsistentiae, three personae.[290] It took a little longer for it to develop; a Roman assembly of churches in the Lateran in the year 649 appears to have translated the Greek term *hypostasis* with the Latin *subsistentia* for the first time: „*unum Deum in tribus subsistentibus.*"[291]
The problems that the Latin West had with the Cappadocian formula are naturally not only linguistic in nature: The talk, adopted in the East, of the three hypostases there had the (tritheistic) overtone of „concrete substance" in contrast to the universal essence; however, out of the inherited soteriological

---

[286] Cf. *Epist. 15 ad Damasum*.
[287] Luise Abramowski, „Zur Trinitätslehre des Thomas von Aquin," *ZThK* 92 (1995): 473, with reference to Augustine, *De trin.* VII, 4, 9.
[288] *De trin.* V, 8, 9-10 (German: BKV, 2nd series, Vol. XIII [Munich, 1935], pp. 200-201.
[289] Cf. L. Abramowski, loc. cit., 473.
[290] Ibid., 474; cf. below 6.4.
[291] TzT 2.1, No. 58.

constraints, one was more readily prepared to accept the deficits in these concepts, since what one was looking for, after all, was somehow to establish the „reality" of the Trinity. Since the Latin theologians did not have this interest, they took exception to the threefold substantiality which could encroach upon the unity of the *unus deus*. Nevertheless, the Eastern formulas – in uncertain translation – were adopted.

6.3 Augustine's Doctrine of the Trinity

With his theology *Augustine* brought up the Latin-Christian mentality in a classical manner and profoundly influenced the subsequent Western development, which was based on Latinity. This is also true for his ideas about the Trinity which – as it will be shown – although aiming to preserve the monotheism, frequently brought about the opposite effect in terms of the history of their impact.

6.3.1 The Taking of the One God as a Starting Point

Augustine's „seat in life" for his reflections on the Trinity is the tension between the Latin soteriological interests focused on the one God, and the tradition from the East of the triadic framework. Although he worked on his treatise „On the Trinity," *De trinitate*, for around twenty years, from 399 to 419, for him it was more a question of an intellectual challenge: He wants to theologically „solve" the problem of a reconciliation of unity and trinity in God that had been posed for him by the tradition to which he considered himself to be bound – the *„fides"* – in a form anticipating the later Scholastic methods and the Middle Ages,[292] *„fides quaerens intellectum."*[293] In the final chapter of his Trinity book *Augustine* formulates this connection quite clearly: „I have brought myself into line with these rules of faith (*regula fidei*) as well as I could and to the extent that you (God, K.-H. O.) have given me the ability to do so; I have sought you and demanded to see with my understanding that

---

[292] The structure of argumentation here also applies for the reception of Eastern Christology, which is why one can quite well consider ancient Latin theology as already the beginning of the Middle Ages. Cf. the division made in the present author's *Fundamentalchristologie*, loc. cit. (1986); Kurt Flasch also reckons in a similar way in his book, published in the same year, *Das philosophische Denken im Mittelalter. Von Augustin zu Macchiavelli* (Stuttgart, 1986), „Augustinus zum Mittelalter."

[293] R. Seeberg, *Lehrbuch der Dogmengeschichte*, Vol. 2, loc. cit., p. 154, says: „It is not the Greek theology, nor is it really the Nicene Synod that is decisive for him, but the authority of the text that he is attempting to justify on a rational basis." This is only correct if one wishes to describe the intentions of Augustine. But he, in fact, is reading the text from the point of view of the later Greek theology; otherwise he would not have had any problems.

which I believed (*desideravi intellectu videre quod credidi*)."[294] However, a soteriological interest cannot be established in him; on the contrary, one has basically just to look at his argumentation to see that it bothers him, though he does not dare to contest it.

He takes as his starting point – unlike the Cappadocians, who are here representative of the Hellenistic-Christian mentality – not just the (abstract) unity of God, but the one („concrete") God. His conversion to Christianity was combined with the turning away from Manicheism, thus from a dualistic thinking, in favor of the turning towards this one Christian God; at the same time, this change was also associated in an essential way with his contact with the Neoplatonism, which had at that time become known in Italy, and its conception of God as a pure and simple unity.

Augustine calls God „a single reality" and „a simple and unchanging substance"[295] – here it becomes clear why he cannot speak of „three substances": *substantia* and *essentia* are for him synonymous terms. However, for him God is just as much a *trinitas*, which *is* the „one, sole and true God" (*unus et solus et verus deus*)[296] and nevertheless does not abolish God's simplicity[297]: „Namely, the Father is God, the Son is God, the Holy Spirit is God, so – no one doubts that these are statements with regard to the substance – so do we still not call this sublime Trinity three gods, but only *one* God."[298] *Everything* that one can say about God applies only for his one substance. „Accordingly, the triune God is *one* substance, *one* nature, *one* divinity, *one* majesty and *one* glory. ... He possesses *one* effect and *one* will."[299] *Augustine* rejects the Cappadocian conception – more specifically that of *Gregory of Nyssa* – which compares the Trinity to three human persons who belong to one species man, and which allocates to the three hypostases different economic functions. In God there are also no qualitative or accidental differences; this would abolish his unity – quite apart from the fact that in God all „qualities" are identical with His substance.[300] And there is also only *one* action of God outwards; even the Incarnation is one indivisibly mutual activity of Father, Son and Spirit,[301] thus of God; the entire Trinity assumed humanity

---

[294] *De trin.* XV, 18, 51, *oratio* (CCL, XVI, 2, 534).

[295] *De trin.* XV, 17 (German: TzT 2.1, No. 111).

[296] *De trin.* I, 2, 4 (CCL, XVI, 1.31).

[297] *De civ. dei* XI, 10; cf. *de trin.* V, 7, 9; 11, 12; VIII, 1.

[298] *De trin.* V, 8, 9 (German: BKV, 2nd series, Vol. XIII, p. 199).

[299] R. Seeberg, *Lehrbuch der Dogmengeschichte*, Vol. 2, loc. cit., p. 155.

[300] Cf. *De trin.* V, 5, 6.

[301] *De trin.* II, 5, 9: „Sic ergo intelligat illam *incarnationem* et *ex virgine* nativitatem in qua filius intelligitur missus una eademque operatione patris et filii inseparabiliter esse factam, non undique separato spiritu sancto. ..." (CCL, XVI, 1, 91): „So may he (anyone who has objections, K.-H. O.) therefore accept that the Incarnation and the birth from the Virgin, in which the Son is recognized as having been sent, occurs through one and the same action of Father and Son in an indivisible way, and this is not separate from the Holy Spirit."

(Jesus).³⁰² The economy is in all of its aspects brought about by the one God and not by the „persons" – to whom one can only *appropriate*, attribute, it in an untrue, inauthentic way.

Reinhold Seeberg accurately summarizes the conception of *Augustine*: „Accordingly, one could say that Augustine strongly felt the elements that (for us, K.-H. O.) converge in the concept of the one personal God. This concept itself was formed as little by him as by another ancient thinker."³⁰³ In this regard, *Augustine*, so to speak, reestablished the original monotheism.

6.3.2 The Formalized Etymology or the Relational Conception of the Trinity

If Father, Son and Spirit are no longer economic quantities, but are „from all eternity," an explanation of their peculiarity becomes problematic. This development had begun with *Origen*, who viewed Son and Spirit as innergodly quantities, but who still avoided the problem in that he shifted into the preexistence the economic functions such as the constitution of the world, in an initial pre-temporal creation, and Christology, in the similarly pre-temporal decision of the soul of Jesus for the Logos, and thus carried out various phases in God Himself. Nicaea had taken this route with the doctrine of the *homoousia* of the Son with the Father, but still accepted in God two who after all still had certain differences – though only paternity and filiation – and economic functions. Since the Cappadocians, the Spirit had become integrated in God and the formula of the one nature in three hypostases had become established; although the latter still clearly possessed specific salvation-historical functions, they were also already a part of the one nature of God „beforehand." Now it became necessary to reflect upon their *„eternal"* particularities; here the only thing left to fall back on was the mere concepts of Father, Son and Spirit, which were etymologically interpreted and were already identified by *Gregory of Nyssa* in their formal structure as relational terms.³⁰⁴

Augustine finally *rejected every economic support in describing the particularities of the Trinity*. There is only *one* action of God outwards. In the same way, „qualitative," that is, in God, substantial differences among the Persons were unthinkable.

---

³⁰² *Ep.* 11.2: Everything that the Trinity does is „to be considered as mutual work of the Father, of the Son and of the Spirit. ... From this it appears to follow that the entire Holy Trinity is become man." (German: BKV, 29 [1917], p. 22). In what follows Augustine then discusses the question of how that is to be combined with the appropriation of the becoming-man to the Son.

³⁰³ *Lehrbuch der Dogmengeschichte*, Vol. 2, loc. cit., p. 157.

³⁰⁴ Cf. above 5.3.4.

Nevertheless, as a starting point he had to take what was for him dogma, the three Persons, even though he did not like this term[305] and was unsure in its application.[306] But then in what does each of their peculiarities consist; then how after all would he explain the personal particularities? He, too, was left with nothing else – since in principle in this case nothing else was available anymore – but to fall back on the etymological meaning of Father, Son and Spirit and other honarary Biblical designations as well as on their special formal nature: *on the relational character of these terms*. He therefore taught the Persons as relational „realities."

A second consideration, which resulted from the special nature of the philosophical reflections of the day, may have provided an additional motivation for him to handle things in this way. *Boethius* († 524 or 526) – much later – gives a hint of this. He had intervened in Christological controversies and in the process tried to define the term Person, whose understanding is not yet unambiguous in *Augustine*, as *individua substantia rationa(bi)lis naturae*, as an „individual substance of a spiritual nature."[307] „Person" would thus be spiritual individuality, and this, according to Boethius, existed in Jesus Christ only once: as the Person of the divine Word.[308] Although he also composed an opuscule on the Trinity,[309] he also avoided bringing this definition into play here because that – the three „individualities" – would have a tritheistic understanding as a consequence. Probably a little concerned that others could proceed in a similar manner, he follows *Augustine* and his relational doctrine of the Trinity more closely: „Father, Son and Holy Spirit are not predicated of the Godhead in a substantial way, but otherwise. ... It is, however, clear that (in the divine relationships, K.-H. O.) it is a question of a predication *ad aliquid*. ... One can thus not even ascribe the Trinity to God in a substantial way. ..."[310]

---

[305] Cf. *De trin.* V, 9, 10; VII, 6, 11.

[306] In the last chapter of his Trinity book, Augustine argues that the ternary of the human spirit (cf. below section 6.3.3) are all related to the one human person: „I am he who remembers, understands and loves through these three. ... These three can thus be predicated of one person who has these three, not who is these three. In the simplicity, on the other hand, of that supreme nature that is God, there are, although there is only one God, nevertheless three persons, the Father, Son and Holy Spirit." (*De trin.* XV, 22, 42; German: BKV, 2nd series, Vol. XIV [Munich, 1936], p. 315; cf. also *De trin.* XV, 23, 43). At the latest at this point Augustine could have pondered the divergence between a Trinitarian concept of person and the concept of person related to man, but he does not – he simply leaves the disparity as it is.

[307] Cf. below 6.4.

[308] Cf. by the present author, *Fundamentalchristologie*, loc. cit., p. 294.

[309] *Opuscula Sacra*: Whether Father, Son and Spirit are predicated of the Godhead in a substantial way (c. 520).

[310] German from: *Gotteslehre II*, ed. Herbert Vorgrimler (*Texte zur Theologie, Dogmatik*, Vol. 2.2 [cited as TzT 2.2]), (Graz, Wien, Köln, 1989), No. 113.

Behind these arguments are considerations that *Augustine* had already taken into account; for example, if God is thought entirely as simple and one, then there can be neither substantial nor accidental plurality in Him: „Consequently, if also no statement about God can involve an accidental property since there is no such thing in God, yet not every statement about Him involves a substantial property. ... Therefore, even if Father and Son are different, there still exists no substantial difference."[311] In order, nevertheless, to be able to speak of a Trinity, the concept of relation offers its services: „For the determinations Father and Son do not involve the substance, but a relationship."[312] This describes an *esse ad* or, as *Boethius* says, an *esse ad aliquid*, that is, a „being *in relation to* (something)." According to the philosophical thinking of the day, which formed its concepts on the basis of present existing or cosmic beings, such a relation did not affect the being itself, the substance, and also represents no quality of a being. This can be illustrated with the help of an example: A brown, four-legged wooden table of a certain size and construction, for example, changes neither its „substance" nor its qualities whenever it changes its spatial relationship – whether it is standing in a room or outside in front of the door – or its function – whether it serves as a dinner table or as a desk; „a relational determination (is) not substantial."[313] This would look different in the case of a – now widely-held – understanding of relation which considers it from a human perspective, hence *intersubjectively*: intersubjective (personal, social, or other) relations – in friendship, love, hate, responsibility, etc. – change the subjects profoundly. For *Boethius* and *Augustine*, however, by means of the concept of relation „realities" could be described that apparently do not affect the being of God. It thus serves the concern that the unity of God continue to be understood as completely *simple* and *untouched* by *plurality*; it was supposed to safeguard and substantiate the monotheism – despite the talk of Father, Son and Spirit – in a conceptual, or more precisely, in a theological-philosophical way.

Therefore, Augustine argues: „The statements, however, which in a characteristic way involve each separate person in the Trinity, express no absolute reality, but the relationship of the three persons to each other or their relationship to the Creation."[314] Or in another passage: „Father is thus a relational expression, likewise Source or any other designations. ... Furthermore, Son is a relational expression, likewise Word and Image,"[315] and Spirit is also „a relational designation since the Holy Spirit includes a relation

---

[311] *De trin.* V, 5, 5 (German: BKV, 2nd series, Vol. XIII, pp. 192-193).

[312] Ibid. V, 5, 6 (German: ibid., p. 193).

[313] Augustine, *De trin.* V, 7, 8 (German: ibid., p. 196).

[314] Ibid. V, 11,12 (German: ibid., p. 203). On this „relationship to the Creation" one can subscribe to the observation of R. Seeberg (loc. cit., p. 159): „But this side does not in any case serve as a point of orientation in the considerations; this side maintains itself as a whole within the ‚immanent Trinity.'"

[315] *De trin.* V, 13, 14 (German: loc. cit., pp. 205-206).

to Father and Son."³¹⁶ The Trinitarian concept of relation is thus, first of all, the formal-logical structure of all of the symbolic concepts available for the description of the trinity, above all, of Father, Son and Spirit; secondly, it serves *Augustine* to ward off all interpretations of the trinity as substantial and thus to defend the monotheism. The concept of relation seems to be the last possible chance to document a trinity linguistically without pluralizing the simplicity of God.

The latter intention was, at any rate, not achieved: The Trinity ought, after all according to the tradition which was deemed to be normative, to represent a divine reality, and in such a way, *Augustine* adds, that the Trinity *is one* God.³¹⁷ In addition, however, this concept results in an aporia: How can mere relations, which after all are relations *of someone/something to someone/ something*, constitute their starting and reference points, the persons, in the first place? If there are no „persons" in God – aside from the relations – but the relations *are* the persons, how can that be conceived? Who/what then has a relation to whom/what since the „whom/what" without relation does not exist? Pointing to the mystery of God is out of place here because the processes and reflections which have led to the Trinitarian application of the concept of relation are thoroughly understandable at every step and from every point of view; instead, it can be seen that the new conceptualization of the Trinity simply does not accomplish what it was intended to accomplish.

The insufficiency of concepts and definitions is nothing but simple logical insufficiency and in no way a reference to a divine mystery. Much more, the conceptual inadequacy is grounded in the insolubility of the „subject matter": to combine the trinity required from the standpoint of the assimilated Christian theology of the East, a trinity which in the meantime had lost its economic grounds, with the West's *one* God and the simplicity of His substance in such a way that it is *not nothing* and nevertheless does not damage the simplicity of God – that is an aporetic task.

6.3.3 The (So-called) Psychological Doctrine of the Trinity

The *imago idea* played a major role in ancient theology: the world and man in particular are God's „image"; in this the statement from Gen. 1.27 – otherwise than in the contexts of the Old Testament³¹⁸ – was fundamentally understood in the sense of a natural analogy. It was therefore also obvious for *Augustine* to

---

[316] Ibid. V, 11, 12 (German: ibid., pp. 203-204).

[317] Cf. *De trin.* I, 2, 4.

[318] According to the Old Testament understanding, the image character of man is based on the notion that in his role in history he resembles Yahweh: Like the latter and in his behalf he rules over creation and takes part in the kingdom of God over history; he participates in the *kabod Yahweh*.

look, for the purposes of the Trinitarian conception of God, for comparable *ternaries*, „trinities," in creation.

He was very strongly influenced by the conceptions of Neoplatonism. Nevertheless, he does not share its conceptions of an emanative connection between God and the cosmos; God is not the immanent world principle, but stands, as in the Bible, as the Other vis-à-vis creation. *Augustine* thus understands the process of creation according to the model of the work of a craftsman who shapes the work according to his plans. At any rate, God's creating goes a ways beyond the action of a craftsman: He also creates – from nothing – the substratum, which He then forms. This is the reason there is no natural kind of analogy between God and creation; God is *causa exemplaris* (not *formalis*) of His creation. The gap between God and creature is infinite.

Consequently, *Augustine* knows that the analogies cannot be used without restriction: „The Trinity is therefore one thing in its own existence, and the image of the Trinity is another in another (in creaturely, K.-H. O.) being." It is after all only an image. „In that supreme Trinity ... there exists such an indivisibility that, whereas a trinity of men cannot be called one man, that Trinity is called one God."[319] For this reason *Augustine* in *De trinitate* avoids drawing any of those comparisons from cosmic reality which had earlier on already become common and which he had also made use of,[320] just as he avoids the obvious references to the threefold social realities, e.g. father, mother, child, etc. He chooses his analogies from the area that one then called „psychology," hence from human intellectual life, analogies that are related to the *one* human representative, the „person," and then has trouble using them to argue that in God on the contrary these ternaries are supposed to make the *three* „persons" understandable.

Augustine mentions a series of such trinities which basically always mean the same thing: „being, knowing and desiring" (*esse, nosse, velle*)[321], „memory, understanding and will" (*memoria, intelligentia, voluntas*)[322], „mind, love, knowledge" (*mens, amor, notitia*)[323], which are all *one* life,[324] or he compares the relations with human self-consciousness in which the mind is both subject and object: „in this way a trinity is made (*fit*) from the memory, the inner

---

[319] *De trin.* XV, 23, 43 (German: BKV, 2nd series, Vol. XIV, p. 316).

[320] Cf. *De fide et symb.* 9, 17: Augustine speaks of a *spring*, which is not the *river* or a *trough*. „And yet there are not three waters, but we are speaking of only one. One must only be careful not to equate the inexpressible substance of the majesty of God with the visible and physical water in the spring, the river and the trough. ..." (German from: Aurelius Augustinus, *Drei Bücher über den Glauben. De fide*, trans. Carl Johann Perl [Aurelius Augustinus' Werke in deutscher Sprache, ed. C.J. Perl], [Paderborn, 1968], p. 27).

[321] *Confessiones* XIII, 11, 12 (Augustinus, *Confessiones. Bekenntnisse*. Latin and German. Introd., trans. and annot. Joseph Bernhart [München, 1955], p. 768).

[322] *De trin.* X, 11, 18 (CCL, XVI,1, p. 330).

[323] Ibid. IX, 4, 4 (CC, XVI, 1, p. 297).

[324] Ibid. X, 11, 18: *non sunt tres vitae sed una vita* or *una substantia* (CCL, XVI, 1, p. 330).

regard and the will which connects the two of them,[325] and he continues, „Now in the case of these three there no longer exists any difference in substance"[326] or God does not fall „apart into the trinity ..., rather it is one single reality that includes all these activities in itself ...; it is indeed a simple and unchanging substance."[327]

Although *Augustine* wants to make a trinity in God understandable with these analogies, he is aware of the inadequacy of the comparisons. In his later reception, however, in medieval times and in the modern age, they did serve to make the threefold relationships a little clearer, and reinforced the tendency to outline more sharply in God the differences between the persons and thereby to reinforce the trinity more than *Augustine* had intended.

6.3.4 The Spirit as Bond of Love

With *Augustine*, the West basically could have again come closer to monotheism; the soteriological reasons for a second and third hypostasis were foreign to the Latin tradition. And in fact there is often in medieval times and in the modern age a soteriological concentration on *God*, who created the world, revealed and incarnated Himself, and works in the church and steers history to its destination.

Nevertheless, there arose in the Latin West two Trinitarian conceptual models which would once again more strongly jeopardize the monotheism; *Augustine* and *Boethius*[328] brought them into play, almost unintentionally and in their sense, in any case, counterproductively.

In two texts *Augustine* expounded upon the previously customary determinations of the Holy Spirit,[329] by attributing to it the task of producing *harmony* (concordia) and a *connection* between Father and Son.[330] Similarly, in *De trinitate* he says: „Thus the Holy Spirit is an ineffable community (communio) of Father and Son."[331]

---

[325] Ibid. XI, 3, 6 (CCL, XVI, 1, p. 340.)

[326] Ibid. (German: BKV, 2nd series, Vol. VIV, p. 104).

[327] *De trin.* XV, 17, 28 (German: BKV, 2nd series, Vol. XIV, pp. 297-298).

[328] Cf. below 6.4.

[329] Here I am following two articles by Luise Abramowski: (1) „Zur Trinitätslehre des Thomas von Aquin," in *Zeitschrift für Theologie und Kirche* 92 (1995), 466-480, more specifically, the „Excursus" contained therein (468-477), and (2) „Der Geist als ‚Band' zwischen Vater und Sohn – ein Theologoumenon der Eusebianer?" in *ZNW* 87 (1996), 126-132.

[330] Augustine, *De doctr. christ.* I, 5, 5: „in the Holy Spirit is the harmony of the unity (or connection, union) and of the equality" (*in spiritu sancto unitatis aequalitatisque concordia*, CCL, Vol. 23, p. 9).

[331] *De trin.* V, 11, 12 (CCL, XVI, 1, p. 219).

L. Abramowski points to a „fragment of the Oracula chaldaica" (Fragment 31)[332], „a kind of Holy Scripture for the Neoplatonists" (2nd half of the 2nd century), whose (pre-Christian) texts were, via the Neoplatonist *Porphyry* (*Augustine* cites two works of *Porphyry* in *De civitate dei*), also known to the Christians. There is talk in this fragment of how out of the two origins, out of the monad and dyad, „the *bond* of the first Trinity" flows. From this *L. Abramowski* concludes: „This looks like the origin both of the idea of the Holy Spirit as the bond of the Trinity and of the controversial conception of the emergence of the Spirit ex patre *filioque*,"[333] out of the Father *and the Son*.

Previously this conception was only known from a polemic by *Athanasius*, which L. Abramowski sees as being directed against *Eusebius of Caesarea*, „our main source for the ‚oracle philosophy' of Porphyry,"[334] and the Eusebians: „ Moreover, the Spirit does not connect the Word with the Father, rather the Spirit conceives from the Word."[335] Thus *Athanasius* took a stand against a Trinitarian version[336] that contradicted his monarchian concerns and is probably the reason that this conception „continued to make no headway" in the East.[337]

On the basis of his presumptive models Augustine – so to speak, unintentionally or even against his other intentions – assigns to the Spirit an *independent*, now totally *inner-trinitarian* function: he is *vinculum*, the *bond* of the community between Father and Son. „Father and Son (are) the primordial basis of the Holy Spirit"[338]; the Spirit includes „in itself a relationship to Father and Son"[339] or is „a certain ineffable community of Father and Son."[340] *Augustine* further specifies what makes up the bond nature of the Spirit: „It is the *love* between Father and Son, „the unity of the two others" and „their love or unity, because (the Spirit) is love."[341] Perhaps this assertion is based upon a theoretical consideration: How can a „band" or „unity" be imagined in the spiritual realm? Here the recourse to love suggests itself. *L. Abramowski*, however, seems to have been able to demonstrate plausibly[342] that in this case he was relying on *literary sources*; she shows that „the Eusebians understood,

---

[332] For details, see L. Abramowski, „Zur Trinitätslehre ...," loc. cit., 470, n. 14.

[333] „Zur Trinitätslehre ...," loc. cit., 470.

[334] Ibid. 471.

[335] Athanasius, *or. 3 c. Arianos* 24 (German: BKV, Vol. 13 [1913], p. 275).

[336] In her second article on this subject, „Der Geist als ‚Band' [„The Spirit as 'Bond'] ...," loc. cit., L. Abramowski shows that this Eusebian version – after 362 – must have undergone a neo-Nicene revision and one would have to presume that Augustine had „a Latin translation of the postulated Trinitarian treatise" in front of him (131-132).

[337] L. Abramowski, „Zur Trinitätslehre ...," loc. cit., 471.

[338] *De trin.* V, 14, 15 (German: BKV, 2nd series, XIII, p. 208).

[339] *De trin.* V, 11, 12 (German: BKV, ibid., p. 204).

[340] Ibid. (German: ibid.).

[341] *De trin.* VI, 5, 7 (German: ibid., pp. 221-222).

[342] As she says in the above-mentioned second article, „Der Geist als ‚Band' ...," loc. cit.

on the basis of easily provided biblical evidence, *our* unity among ourselves as like that of the Holy Spirit and of love; the „bond of love" is the Holy Spirit who works as love and thus as the binding force upon us."[343] This conception, which touches on the economic work of the Spirit *among us* has – now in a neo-Nicene way because immanently related to the Trinity – been „transferred to the intradivine relationship": „the Spirit was now the bond ... (that) united the Logos and the Father."[344] Thus the interpretation of the „bond" as love is probably traceable back to the neo-Nicene transposition of the economic function of the Spirit into God Himself.

Augustine has thereby, at any rate, which must be taken into account, in accordance with his presumptive model, given the Spirit a God-immanent function „only" in the manner also already identifiable among the Cappadocians after their attempts to emphasize the unity of God more strongly: paternity, filiation and breathing/being breathed or proceeding are likewise no longer economic, but intradivine functions; the Spirit is thus, however, *taken out of its merely passive role* by *Augustine*; it is – actively – community, bond, love between Father and Son. Thus the impression is reinforced that it is something like a „subject." The path has now been trodden toward comprehending the Trinity as a community of three subjects in one essence.

One of the most important special features of the Western-Latin doctrine of the Trinity, that namely the Spirit does not proceed from the Father (alone) *through* the Son, but from Father *and* Son *(filioque)* and that a *bond of love* is between the two of them, is thus in all likelihood non-Christian in origin and was probably picked up by *Augustine* because he did not recognize the explosiveness of this conception: that it not only was an *innovation* with regard to the Eastern doctrine of the Trinity – which much later, in the year 1054, became the sole theological grounds for the schism between the Eastern and the Western church – but that it would also necessarily encourage what was for him an unwanted *version of the Trinity as a community of three loving subjects*.

6.4 Boethius' Definition of Person

The Western Roman consul and philosopher Boethius, in his work „Against Eutyches and Nestorius" (*Contra Eutychen et Nestorium*), said what he thought about the different terminologies in the East and West in connection with the Christological and Trinitarian discussions; his remarks show that at the time neither the understanding of the Greek terminology nor its translation into Latin had even to the slightest extent been clarified.[345]

---

[343] Ibid. 130-132.
[344] Ibid. 131.
[345] In *Contra Eutychen et Nestorium* (German: TzT 2.2, No. 112) he suggests that the Greeks had „designated with the word hypostasis the individual subsistence of a rational nature." What he understands under the term subsistence, stemming from Marius Victorinus (cf. above

He believes he can enlist the term person both for the Christology and for the doctrine of the Trinity and he tries to define it: „If person is only found in substances, and indeed only in those blessed with reason; if furthermore every substance is a nature; if finally person is not contained in general concepts, but only in individual essences, then the definition of the person has been found: Person is the individual substance of a rational nature [persona est naturae rationabilis individua substantia]."[346]

On the basis of the further linguistic development in the Latin West, in which *persona* (originally used, in *Tertullian*, in the sense of „role" or „legal representation") gradually – not yet in *Augustine* – became the designation of individuality, and in the context of the Christological discussion, in which a point of unity was sought for Jesus Christ between the two natures, which – in the wake of the Council of Chalcedon – could not be natural, *Boethius* created a definition whose historical impact cannot be overestimated.

Though he perhaps had not so clearly thought through his terminology, his formula provided the stimulus for grounding individuality not – as previously – only as the result of the realization of a universality in matter or its specification by means of accidental properties; for the first time Spirit itself was understood as *per se individual* – later one would say as reflexive, i.e. conscious of itself, etc. With that *Boethius* profoundly influenced the

---

p. 89), he describes – as distinct from substance – in the following way: „The subsistences are in truth contained in the universals [in universalibus]; they assume substance, however, in the individual entities. That is why subsistences that have through individuation acquired substance are properly called hypostases. No one who looks carefully and exactly will consider substance and subsistence to be synonyms. ... And, in fact, whatever has no need of accidents to be able to exist is subsistent. ... Man has an essence (οὐσία), a subsistence (οὐσίωσις), a ὑπόστασις (*substantia*), a πρόσωπον (*persona*); an οὐσία or *essentia* because he is; an οὐσίωσις or *subsistentia* because he does not cling to one subject; a ὑπόστασις or *substantia* because he is the foundation for the rest that is not *subsistentia*; πρόσωπον or person because he is an individual blessed with reason." Boethius then applies these terms to God: „God is οὐσία or essence since God is. ... He is οὐσίωσις, i.e. subsistence, since he subsists without need of anything whatsoever; ... He is substance. Therefore we also say that there is only one οὐσία or οὐσίωσις, i.e. only one essence or subsistence of the Godhead, but three ὑποστάσεις, i.e. three substances." Here it becomes evident that he – unlike Marius Victorinus and the official later Latin version – relates the concept of subsistence, not to the trinity, but to the one God; for the trinity he prefers the term substance which he considers to be semantically identical with hypostasis. But he knows that the Latin church has reservations here. „On the basis of this approach, one could say of the Trinity: one essence, but three substances or persons. If the usage of the church did not prevent us from ascribing three substances to God, then it would obviously be legitimate to designate Him as a substance. ..." Thus he falls back, for the characterization of the trinity, upon the concept of person, even though „the Greeks" speak „much more correctly" of hypostasis.

[346] Ibid. (German: ibid.).

intellectual historical development of Europe all the way up to the later development of individualism and personalism.

In theology, however, his definition set fateful processes into operation: In Christology, *una persona* – as the Latin translation of the one *prósopon* of the symbol of Chalcedon – now had to be understood in the sense of a sole individuality or (in the modern sense) personality of the God incarnate Jesus Christ; after *Boethius* the *una persona* of the divine *verbum* therefore replaces that of the man Jesus.

This Christological application of the concept of person shows that *Boethius* understood the „person" of the Logos in a sense that is so similar to that of a man that there could not be two persons – one divine *and* one human – in Jesus Christ. In other words, in connection with the Trinity he imagined three spiritual individualities. This conception became conviction throughout the West – the Christological „monopersonalism"[347] of European theology.

In the doctrine of the Trinity, *Boethius* – as already explained – nevertheless shrunk back from an application of his definition and once again leaned more heavily on *Augustine*'s relational conceptualization.[348] But this could not prevent the history of reception from developing its own dynamics: the trinity came to be understood more and more in the sense of a (modern) triple personality, a terminology which in the West possessed a long tradition reaching back to *Tertullian* and revived by *Augustine*, but which had now come to be understood in the totally new sense of a threefold spiritual individuality. An inner-godly tritheism became – against the soteriological interests of the West – ever more determining from that point on.

The definition of *Boethius* thus reinforced the trend set in motion by the *Augustinian* conception of the Spirit as the bond of love between Father and Son. Both together allowed a notion to arise according to which *God is a love-community of three subjects.*

---

[347] Cf. by the present author, *Fundamentalchristologie*, loc. cit., e.g., p. 339.
[348] Cf. above p. 92-93.

7. The Consolidation of Western Conceptions of the Trinity in the Middle Ages

The Trinitarian conceptions of the Middle Ages will only be shown here in their basic structures. A presentation of the views of individual epochs or theologians would take up a great deal of space, considering that the Middle Ages encompass a period of more than a thousand years, and if one also adds to this the ancient Latin theology – which would according to the approach probably be correct[349] – then a period even a few centuries longer.

7.1 The Safety of Formulaic Language and the Victory of the Trinitarian Etymology

It corresponded to the Latin mentality as well as to the beginning Scholastic methods to prop up expressions of faith on apparently unambiguous formulas and definitions. This need was complied with by a creed which arose perhaps around 500, probably in Gaul, and which was later incorrectly attributed to *Anthanasius*: the *Symbolum Quicumque* or *Athanasium*. It was highly esteemed throughout the Middle Ages, but even among the reformers – the Anglican Church still uses it in the liturgy today – as well as in the Russian Church.[350]
In it one finds: „We worship the One God in the Trinity and the Trinity in the unity, without confusion of the persons and without separation of the essence. One is namely the person of the Father, another that of the Son, another that of the Holy Spirit. However, Father and Son and Holy Spirit have only one divinity, equal glory, equal eternal majesty. ... Eternal is the Father, eternal the Son, eternal the Holy Spirit. And yet there are not three that are eternal. But One that is Eternal ... thus is the Father Lord, the Son Lord, the Holy Spirit Lord, and yet there are not three Lords, but only One Lord ... thus we are forbidden ... by the Catholic faith to accept three gods or lords." There then follows an explanation of the eternal Trinitarian peculiarities on the basis of the etymological meaning of the corresponding symbolic terms, in the course of which the *filioque* is taught for the Spirit: „The Father is made by no one, neither created nor begotten. The Son is by the Father alone not made, nor created, but begotten. The Holy Spirit is from the Father and from the Son, not made, nor created, nor begotten, but proceeding. ..."[351]
This formulaic language as well as the immanent-etymological interpretation of the Trinity and the *filioque* was also established in Spain. A *synod*, which took place – as the eleventh assembly of the Church in this region – in the year 675

---

[349] Cf. above note 292.
[350] Cf. J. Quasten, „Quicumque," in *LThK²* 8, 937-938.
[351] German: „Das ‚Athanasianische' Glaubensbekenntnis," in Neuner-Roos, No. 915 (my emphasis, K.-H. O.)

in *Toledo*, adopted a *creed* in which the unity of God, similarly to the *Symbolum Quicumque*, is clearly brought out: „We profess and believe that the Holy and ineffable Trinity ..., the One God, possesses by nature one essence, one glory and power." Afterwards, the trinity is elucidated on the basis of its symbolic terms: We profess that the *Father* is not begotten, not created, but unbegotten. ... We also acknowledge the *Son*, who was born out of the substance of the Father without beginning before time and yet was not created. For the Father was never without the Son, the Son never without the Father. And yet the Father is not from the Son in the way the Son is from the Father. ... We also believe that the *Holy Spirit*, the third person in the Trinity, is one and the same God with the Father and the Son: one substance and also one nature. However, that one is not begotten nor created, but proceeds from both and is the spirit of both ... that one proceeds at the same time from both since that one must be seen as the love or the holiness of both."[352]

Towards the end of the symbol the terms Father, Son and Spirit are used even more clearly to explain the eternal Trinity: „Thus, although these three are one, this One is three, yet the peculiarity of each person remains. Proper to the Father is eternity without birth, to the Son eternity with birth, to the Holy Spirit proceeding without birth with eternity. ..."[353]

This „clear" formulaic language is also found in this period among theologians who systematically summarize the prior conceptual results and in medieval times were highly esteemed, above all *Maximus Confessor* († 662) and *John of Damascus* († 750). The latter also explicitly throws into relief the etymological interpretation of the terms Father, Son and Spirit: The Father is from all eternity Father and was never without Son, „[f]or without Son He could not be *called* Father (emphasis mine, K.-H. O.). If he was once without Son, then He was not Father."[354] As an Eastern theologian, however, he teaches the proceeding of the Spirit only from the Father and speaks of the „interpenetration of the hypostases,"[355] of their *perichoresis*.

These examples should suffice. This formulaic language became from now on part of the common heritage of Western Christianity to this day. It itself since that time has neither been called into question nor further developed, but has merely been subjected to various interpretations.

At first, only a few of the works of the ancient theologians on the Trinity – except, above all, those of *Augustine* – were known to the Middle Ages. Over long stretches of time only single sentences were compiled in so-called *catenae* collections and only since the „Carolingian renaissance" were several of the Greek works translated in their entirety into Latin. As a result one knew relatively little about the stages and motivations in the development of the traditional definitions; one knew only the formulas.

---

[352] German: TzT 2.2, No. 59-62.

[353] German: Ibid., No. 69.

[354] „Exact Presentation of the Orthodox Faith," I, 8 (German: TzT 2.2, No. 117).

[355] Loc. cit. (German: loc. cit., No. 118)

A double possibility was thus opened up: On the one hand, an interpretation of the formulas could develop in such a way as to view them in the light of their *own* soteriological interests (cf. the next chapter); on the other, there was the danger of defining older Trinitarian expressions, such as that of the *una essentia* and of the *tres personae*, on the basis of later definitions, for instance, on the basis of *Boethius'* definition of person, and in this way to misunderstand their original content (cf. the chapter after next).

7.2 The „Three – I-Don't-Know-Whats" or the Interest in the One God

The Latin West had a soteriological interest in the One God. This becomes clear, despite the now prevailing triple personality of God, wherever there is nevertheless talk of their being in Him only *one* knowing, *one* will, *one* energy, that is, *one* principle of activity and *one* action outwards.

This is emphasized not only by *Augustine*, who was such a formative influence on the Middle Ages, but also by other theologians and synods in the early Middle Ages. One synod, which took place *in the Lateran in 649* and first employed the term subsistence as the translation of the Greek *hypóstasis*,[356] stresses the „one and the same divinity" and emphasizes the „one nature, essence, ..., will, activity."[357]

There are also difficulties involved with the use of the Trinitarian concept of person. *Anselm* of Canterbury († 1109) unquestionably takes Trinitarian dogma as his point of departure: „Behold, it stands to reason that it profits each man to believe in an ineffable threefold unity and *one* trinity." But then he adds: „And indeed in ‚one' trinity because of the *one* essence, ‚three' however and ‚trinity' because of the *three – I-don't-know-whats*."[358] Here his difficulty in assigning a term to the trinity becomes apparent. Afterwards he enters into the details – „if I were to say ... three persons" – of the traditional conceptual framework: „For one must not take them (the three, K.-H. O.) to be three persons, since several persons all exist in such a way separate from one another that there are necessarily as many substances as there are persons; which one recognizes in the case of several people, who are as many substances existing for themselves as there are persons. Thus just as there are not several substances in the Highest Essence, so are there also not several persons."[359] Nevertheless he, who does not want to call the faith, the *fides*, into question with his intellect, is „only" seeking to know more profoundly how he is to comply with the normative usage. But his dissatisfaction with this terminology and his interest in preserving the unity of God are noticeable.

---

[356] Cf. above pp. 89.

[357] „Condemnation of Fallacies concerning the Trinity" (German: TzT 2.1, No. 58).

[358] *Monologion* 79 (German: TzT 2.2, No. 119, final emphasis mine, K.-H. O.).

[359] Ibid. (German: ibid.).

Peter Lombard († 1160) in his *Sentences* book also quite extensively cites *Augustine*'s objections to the concept of person[360] – but advocates in the Christology a radical monopersonalism – and *Thomas Aquinas* also deals intensively with the difficulties[361]: the term is not Biblical – as a translation of the Greek *prósopon* – derived from the masks in dramas, its equation with *hypóstasis* problematic, etc. On the other hand, however, he regards the „Athanasian Creed," the *symbolum quicumque*,[362] as normative and simply refers back to the notion that „person," when applied to the Divine Person, is something other than in the general understanding of the term. With respect to the Trinity it serves to designate the *original relationships (relationes origenis)*.[363] „The relationship is, however, in the divine (sphere) not to be comprehended as an accidental property that adheres to some entity; it is, on the contrary, subsisting, just as the divine essence subsists."[364]

The problem of how these subsisting relationships do not abolish the simplicity of God is answered by *Thomas* with verbalisms: „*Divine Person*, namely, designates the relation (relatio) *as existing for itself* ..., although that which is existing in the divine nature is nothing else but the divine nature itself."[365] Nevertheless, *Thomas* does manage to formulate an „understanding of persons which gets out beyond an orientation on self-consciousness and self-possession"[366]; his theology is in this respect more subtle and discriminating and more aware of the problems than those of most of the others. However, he does not provide a solution either.

Although he dislikes the term person even in the new application of the concept, he can at least declare it to be – the minimum Thomistic qualification – „adequate": „Accordingly, the following can be said: The meaning of the noun *person* was not yet known before the erroneous establishment of the false doctrines; therefore the noun *person* was also only in use like one of the other nouns used unrelatedly. Later, however, the noun person was brought so far into line that it could be deemed to have a relation, and indeed out of the adequacy of its designation, so that it has precisely this, that it is deemed to be a noun of relation, not only from its use, but also from its meaning."[367] This means nothing else but that the term must continue to be „redefined" until it can at least be considered as adequate in its relational interpretation.

Unfortunately, in Christology *Thomas* also advocated a conception that ascribed no human person to the man Jesus because apparently the person of

---

[360] *Libri IV Sententiarum* I, 2-4.

[361] *Summa theologica* I, q. 29, a. 3 and 4.

[362] Cf. above p. 103-104.

[363] Loc. cit., article 4.

[364] Ibid.

[365] Ibid. (German: TzT 2.2, No. 150).

[366] H. Vorgrimler, „Introduction to the Texts of Thomas Aquinas," in TzT 2.2, No. 149 (p. 69).

[367] Ibid. (German: ibid.).

the *verbum* was then understood as a second person on the same level as that of a man: „Now precisely in the case of all other men, body and soul are combined in order for themselves (per se) to exist (and to form a person, K.-H. O.), in contrast to Christ, where they are united in order to be borne by a higher person. Because of that, no new bearer of His human nature arises in Christ from body and soul, but both merge together into one person who already previously existed."[368] With this Thomas basically frustrates his own distinctions with regard to the divine Persons; these are after all conceived of as so analogous to men that that of the *verbum* would not have been able to coexist with a person of Jesus.

It was probably not possible to say more at this time. One could no longer push the formulas aside and replace them with other conceptual frameworks – but one also apparently knew of none better. One *had* to speak of some kind of „three – I-don't-know-whats" or other. Since the historical material was neither accessible nor was it possible to think about it already in a historico-critical way, nor for this reason could anyone guess what was meant by the three and why they existed, one kept to the traditional way of speaking.

The really felt functionlessness of the trinity becomes even more evident where it is not itself directly thematized and duly and Scholastically discussed, but where, in accordance with the initial history and motivating factors of its origins, it would in a special way have had to have been brought up: in the Christology. In this area it often turns out that in medieval (and even modern) theology, where it is primarily a soteriological question of the redemption from our sins or the justification, the *deus-incarnatus* is the focus of attention[369]: Jesus Christ redeemed us from our sins or justified us because he was both man and *God*, could take our sin upon himself and yet not be seized by it, suffer in our place and also – because he was *God* – make amends. Even the actual giving of justification to individual people by means of mercy is usually considered less a specific activity of the Spirit as the everlasting will *of God*, who saves whomever He wishes. The appropriation of Incarnation and justification to hypostases of their own was indeed retained, but was not a central concern for one's own faith.

Thus it can be concluded that the dogma of the Trinity, though preserved, professed and Scholastically reflected upon at great conceptual pains, played – in this respect at least – *no soteriological role*; Christianity for many theologians would have functioned in its central doctrines even if God had been imagined as undifferentiated. The doctrine of the Trinity moved nothing and nobody, and the trinity of persons or of – for the simple faithful at any rate incomprehensible – relationships, left behind perplexity.

---

[368] *Summa theologica* III, *q.* 2, *a.* 5, *ad* 1 (German: TzT 4.2, No. 181).
[369] Cf. by the present author, *Fundamentalchristologie*, loc. cit., Part III.3; Part IV.1.

7.3 The Threefold Community of Love

In another developmental line, however a Trinitarian conception evolved in the Middle Ages which, to be sure, made the trinity understandable and even soteriologically meaningful, but which more than threatened the unity of God. The motivation for this conception was, on the one hand, the concept of person, which was in the meantime more and more, and even more intensely, grasped in the sense of *Boethius*'s definition, on the other hand, *Augustine*'s doctrine of the Spirit as the bond of love between Father and Son.

7.3.1 Three Self-Conscious Persons in God

In the Middle Ages two Latin terms were available for designating the trinity in God: *subsistentia* as the translation of the Greek *hypóstasis* and *persona* as an equivalent for *prósopon* and, at the same time, *for hypóstasis*. The word subsistence was very abstract and at best usable in the technical terminology of theology, but not in preaching and the liturgy. It thus plays a subordinate role, and where it is taken up it is explained from the point of view of the *Augustinian* relations. If the term was supposed to introduce independent associations into the Trinitarian speculation, then only in the sense that it too suggested the substantiality of the relations from the meaning of the word; but in any case theology had no choice but to assert this, since everything that is in God must subsist in His essence.

More important than this was the term *persona*, which through the definition of *Boethius* was ever more clearly viewed as a subject-like spiritual individuality. The previously mentioned[370] Eleventh Council of Toledo in the year 675 already understood the concept of person in this sense; it distinguishes in God between „the same *(one)*" – the person – and „the same *(thing)*" – the nature or the essence: „Although we have thus said that these three persons are *one* God, one can still not say the Father is the same *(one)* as the Son, or the Son the same *(one)* as the Father, or the Holy Spirit is the Father or the Son. The Father, namely, is not the same *(one)* as the Son, nor is the Holy Spirit the same *(one)* as the Father or the Son, although of course the Father is the same *(thing)* as the Son, the Son the same *(thing)* as the Father, the Father and the Son the same *(thing)* as the Holy Spirit: by nature *one* God."[371]

Here a similar development becomes apparent in a manner parallel to the reception of the Christological formula of the two natures in the *una persona*. The natures are comprehended more and more as „whatnesses" which come together in the one person, the „who" of the divine Logos/*verbum*; the human nature of Jesus is – viewed for itself – non-personal (anhypostatic) and first gains personality with its assumption by the person of the *verbum* in whom it is

---

[370] Cf. above 7.1.
[371] German: TzT 2.1, No. 66.

„enhypostatized." Obviously, the divine person of the Son was thus understood in such away that next to it a person of the man Jesus would violate the formula of the *una persona*; the divine person corresponds to a human person.

This line of thought can also be demonstrated in the *Creed of Toledo*. „Of the three persons (in God) only the person of the Son has ... received from the Holy Virgin a true man without sin. ... We are standing by two natures in this Son of God, one of divinity, one of humanity. ... If we maintain that there are two natures in the Son, we will in any case not therefore propose that there are two persons in him – to avoid having, far from it, a quaternity come to the Trinity. God the Word, namely, has not assumed the Person of a man, but (his) nature, and has taken up into the eternal person of the Godhead the time-bound substance of the flesh."[372] Thus the divine persons are thought of as being on the same level as the human person of Jesus, so that the latter, if it were to exist, would because of its connection with the *verbum* make the Trinity into a quaternity.

Taken up in the wake of *Augustine* is furthermore the relational interpretation of the divine persons. As it was to be expected from a simplifying reception, however, one did not understand the aporetic character of the *Augustinian* views, according to which the relations would first of all constitute the persons. These relationships were much more easily and more plausibly imagined were they – just as for people – to exist between already existent persons. Of course, even here *Augustine* himself had already provided points of contact, above all with his theory of the Spirit as the bond of love. Now, however, his restrictions are for the most part set aside. Thus it says in the *Creed of the Eleventh Synod of Toledo*: „In the names of the persons that express a relationship, the Father is related to the Son, the Son to the Father, the Holy Spirit to both. ... Namely, insofar as the Father is Father, He is not so to Himself, but to the Son. And insofar as the Son is Son, he is not so to himself, but to the Father. In the same way the Holy Spirit is not related to itself, but to the Father and to the Son."[373]

The Trinity thus appears as a trinity of „who's," of Father, Son and Spirit, who stand in relationship to one another, through the Spirit even „as the love ... of the two of them,"[374] of Father and Son. With this the number three acquires a graphic reality: „This Holy Trinity, which is the one and true God, does not leave aside the *number*, but is not grasped by the number. In the relationship of the persons, the number becomes apparent. In the divine essence, however, one can detect nothing countable."[375] What else does that mean but that the number has to do with three „who"-nesses, whereas the „what"-ness is only undifferentiatedly *one*?

In spite of these conceptual determinations, there was a new Christological attempt towards the end of the 8th century in Spain, the so-called Spanish

---

[372] German: TzT 4.1, No. 39.
[373] German: TzT 2.1, Nos. 63 and 64.
[374] German: ibid., No. 62.
[375] German: ibid., No. 65.

adoptionism, in which the humanity of Jesus Christ was given a stronger emphasis.[376] This was refuted by *Alcuin* († 804), the „court theologian" of *Charlemagne*, and he let his conception be confirmed by a *council in Frankfurt* in the year 794.

He argues in this connection entirely on the basis of *Boethius'* concept of person. He understands the two natures of Jesus Christ as thinglike, like the body and soul of a man: „Just as any given man is a person out of a soul of spirit and flesh, so is Christ a person: the Word and the man. ..."[377] In the process it is clear for him that this person is the „person of the Son of God." „Namely, in the assumption of the flesh by God the person of the man was lost, not the nature."[378] These theses were officially legitimized by the *council in Frankfurt* in 794: „Thus did the person of the Son remain in the Trinity, to which person the human nature was added in order that a person would also be God and man."[379] There was thereby established a Christological *monopersonalism* as well as, for the Trinitarian person, an analogy, if not in fact a conceptual congruence, with the human person.

The courses were now set for the entire later history both of Christology and of the doctrine of the Trinity. In the years to come there were only more detailed reflections on what a person is, reflections which usually intensified these tendencies. *Hugh of Saint Victor* († 1141) defined the person as a „self-conscious spirit" (*spiritus rationalis ... per se discernens se*),[380] and the Word was this already eternally even „before this union" with Jesus: „By no means did the Word begin to be a person when it began to be man; rather it took on man (Jesus, K.-H. O.) so that man would begin to be a person. ... This is why the Word, the person, took on man, not a person, but the nature."[381] Here it becomes clear that *Hugh* pictures three self-conscious subjects in the Trinity.

To be sure, more subtle theologians were quite aware of the problems caused by this and tried to offset them with learned discussions. *Richard of Saint Victor* († 1173), for example, is of the opinion that in the case of the Trinity in God it is „better" to speak of „existences than ... substances or subsistences"[382] and also considers *Boethius'* definition of person to be inadequate,[383] but his own suggestion can by no means remove the aporia: „It would perhaps be simpler and more understandable to say ‚Person is a through-itself-existing, in a specific unique way rationalistic existence.'"[384] It is not apparent how this formulation would be better able to avoid an inner-godly tritheism.

---

[376] Cf. by the present author, *Fundamentalchristologie*, loc. cit., pp. 337-338

[377] *Against the Heresies of Felix (of Urgel)*; German: TzT 4.2, No. 165.

[378] *Seven Books against Felix of Urgel* (German: TzT 4.2, No. 166).

[379] German: TzT 4.1, No. 40.

[380] *De sacramentis christianae fidei* II, 1, 11 (MPL 176 [1880], 406 C).

[381] Ibid. II, 1, 9 (German: TzT 4.2, No. 172).

[382] *De trinitate* IV, 20 (German: TzT 2.2, No. 131).

[383] Ibid. IV, 24.

[384] Ibid. IV, 24 (German: TzT 2.2, No. 135).

Thomas Aquinas († 1274) also discusses the difficulty in ascribing reality to the three persons in spite of the simple unity of God and in doing so has recourse to the relational interpretation of the concept of person by *Augustine*: „However, whereas the relations inhere in the created things as something added, so are they in God the divine nature itself. From this *it follows that in God nature and person are in their reality not something different and that nevertheless the persons are really distinguished from one another*. The person, namely, designates the relation as something which in divine nature exists for itself. However, if one compares the relation with the essence, it does not differ really, but only conceptually; if, on the contrary, one compares it with the opposing relation, there falls to it on the strength of the confrontation a real difference. And thus there remains one essence and three persons."[385]

These arguments have the advantage of problematizing a far too simple understanding of the three divine persons. In the last one, however, *Thomas* offers only mutually excluding propositions, which cannot be otherwise either as long as the immanent trinity is to have some form of reality. Moreover, his reservations with regard to the trinity could be taken more seriously if in the Christology he had not supported a monopersonalism which then in fact viewed the person of the *verbum* in competition with a human person of Jesus.[386]

In later history, up to the present day, there have also been many original interpretations of a unity and trinity in God, and some of them are quite profound and even fascinating to read. However, they all take as a starting point a Christian legitimacy or, to be more precise, normativeness of the Trinitarian dogma and – for the purposes of our inquiry – do not get us any further.

7.3.2 The „Exultation of Selfless Love"

The notion, taken over by the Eusebians from Neoplatonic roots, that a third hypostasis – the Spirit – proceeds from the first and second hypostases and combines them, had been picked up by *Augustine* and became the source of the *filioque* of the Latin doctrine of the Trinity. In the same way, *Augustine* had already found the Eusebian doctrine that the Spirit was a bond of love among the faithful in the form of a neo-Nicene redefinition according to which this love was interpreted intradivinely; thus the Spirit was for him the bond of love between Father and Son.[387]

This Western expansion of the doctrine of the Trinity taken over from Eastern theology prevailed more and more in the early Middle Ages and is already found in the *Symbolum Quicumque* which was presumably written in Gaul

---

[385] *Summa theol.* I, *q.* 39, *a.* 1, *responsio* (German: TzT 4.2, No. 183).
[386] Cf. above 7.1.
[387] Cf. above 6.3.4.

around 500.[388] The *filioque* was also adopted in Spain at a very early date: at the First Synod of Toledo (475?), the third (589), fourth (633), sixth (638) and, as discussed above,[389] at the Eleventh Synod of Toledo (675).[390] Likewise, in Spain the *filioque* appears for the first time to have been added to the creed ascribed to the First Council of Constantinople[391] and to have been prayed during the Mass. Even *Charlemagne* „had it ... prayed in his Aachen chapel after the Gospel."[392] Although there was also resistance to this practice, the *filioque* was able to gain general acceptance and became, in the year 1054, the theological grounds for the schism between the Eastern and the Western Church. Occasionally the function of the Spirit, which proceeds from the Father *and from the Son*, was also beyond that described in official documents as the „love ... of the two of them."[393]

Thus guidelines were established for European theology which it could no longer do without and which it had no desire to do without. Precisely the *filioque* and the predication of the Spirit as the „bond of love" between Father and Son opened up the possibility of understanding the entire Trinity aside from all the salvation-historical functions – the Eastern doctrine of a proceeding of the Spirit *from the Father through the Son* almost necessarily drew attention to the economic aims of the „process" – in an exclusively immanent way and of giving this immanent conception a plausible sense.

Two examples should illustrate the direction taken by the argumentation: The already mentioned early Scholastic theologian, *Richard* of Saint.Victor,[394] almost graphically traced the Trinity back to love: „Because for so many reasons we are denied further evasion, we must admit that each person in the Godhead is so magnanimous that it does not wish to have for itself any unshared riches or joys. And since God is so powerful, ... one must conclude that the Trinity of the divine persons is purely and simply necessary. ... If a god were only one person, then he would have no one with whom to share the wealth of his magnanimity. And in turn he would be eternally deprived of the sweet happiness with which intimate love could have enriched him. If, however, the full goodness does not permit the supremely good God jealously to hold back his riches, so too does the full bliss not permit the entirely blissful God to go without them and to the glorification of His majesty He is just as pleased magnanimously to squander them as to enjoy them. From this it is once again evident to you *how impossible it is that in God one person of the community could do without the others. Supposing, however, that there were only one companion there, then although God would be able to squander his*

---

[388] Cf. above 7.1.

[389] Cf. above 7.1 and 7.3.1.

[390] Cf. J. Gill, „Filioque," in *LThK*² 4, 126.

[391] Cf. above 5.2.2.2 and 5.4.

[392] J. Gill, loc. cit., 126.

[393] Cf., e.g., the *Symbolum Quicumque*, above 7.1.

[394] Cf. above 7.3.1.

glorious abundance, he would have no one to whom he could communicate the rapture of total love. However, there is absolutely nothing more gladdening, nothing more heartwarming than the exultation of selfless love. Anyone who has no fellow companion in the reception of the love accorded to him would have to experience such exultation alone. *Therefore the communion in love can only take place if there are three persons.*"[395]

There can be no more drastic justification for the necessity of the trinity in God. *Herbert Vorgrimler* sets things straight: „Augustine had hinted at the notion, but did not take it any further due to the danger of tritheism." But when he says that Richard's approach is „the most original since Augustine,"[396] that is probably going too far, because basically this unpacking of the *Augustinian* figure of speech was to be expected as soon as the three divine persons were viewed in analogy with three human subjects and the theological inhibitions relating to the unity of God had disappeared. The conceptions of *Richard* are not so much original as popular and simplistic.

In any case, the Trinity now no longer seems to be an aporetic or at least hard-to-interpret idea. *This* Trinity is extremely plausible, leaves no questions unanswered and completely explains everything immanently and logically; on top of that it is – lovable.

Bonaventure († 1274) adopted these arguments and even amplified them; through him they were taken up into the theology of the Franciscans, one of the two – next to the Dominicans – large theological schools of the High Middle Ages. In his „Itinerary of the Soul to God," he writes: „For ,of the good we say that it communicates itself.' Thus the highest good communicates itself in the most perfect way. The highest self-communication must, however, be real and intimate, substantial and personal, natural and voluntary, free and necessary, faultless and perfect. Hence, if in the highest good a real process in conformity with its essence had not for all eternity taken place and if there were not *through begetting and breathing* a hypostasis equally sublime as that creating it – an eternal corollary principle of the eternal principle – *hence a lover and a fellow lover*, one begotten and one breathed, namely, Father, Son and Spirit, then it would not be the highest good. ..." In what follows *Bonaventure* expresses the opinion that „the Trinity of the Father, Son and Holy Spirit" is „necessarily given."[397]

Richard of Saint Victor and *Bonaventure* thus derive the Trinitarian structure of God compellingly from the proposition that the good must communicate or squander itself („*bonum est diffusivum sui*"[398]); in addition to that, they apply

---

[395] *De trinitate* III, 14 (German: TzT 2.2, No. 128; emphasis mine, K.-H. O.).

[396] H. Vorgrimler, „Introduction to the Texts of Richard of St. Victor," in TzT 2.2, No. 128 (p. 44).

[397] *Itinerarium mentis in Deum* VI (German: TzT 2.2, No. 139 [Material in single quotes from Dionysius the Areopagite, the Pseudo-Dionysius, *De caelesti hierarchia* 4]; emphasis mine, K.-H. O.).

[398] Ps.-Dionys, cf. the previous note.

to the – pre-given – divine persons popular conceptions concerning interpersonal love in accordance with the model of a community of father, mother and child and of the minimal form of any community (*tres faciunt collegium*); to Western stereotypes of an ideal mode of existence – who in this country (it would be different, for example, in Far Eastern religious contexts) would like to live in permanent solitude? – are projected into God. It was possible to proceed like this because the application of the concept of person in the sense of *Boethius* had become established and the Western expansion of the Trinitarian dogma to include the *filioque* and the doctrine of the Spirit as the „bond of love" had created a basis for it. Even though it is not a question in the case of this model of an original, but rather of a trivializing variation which smoothes over the tensions between unity and trinity, still one could say that in the end result *a fully new form of Trinitarian doctrine has arisen*. Without any reference to salvation history, out of which by means of hypostatization the most important economic functions of the doctrine of the Trinity had resulted, the Trinity is now made plausible in a totally immanent way; the aporetic status of the doctrine, which had first arisen with *Origen* out of the shift in focus from the economy to immanence, is thus ended. Why there are – indeed why there *must be* – three persons in God is now obvious.

These persons – still disregarding their nearer definitions – could now no longer be understood otherwise than in analogy with three human subjects and subjectivities: comrades and fellow comrades, lovers, loved ones and fellow loved ones – terms of this kind permit no other conclusion. That these three must not abolish the unity of God, although it was (and is) vehemently acknowledged verbally, has not at all led to a correction or even to the problematization of this approach.

7.4 Excursus: The Triadic Self-Fulfillment of God[399]

The theology of *John Scotus Erigena* († before 880), one of the most important thinkers of the Middle Ages, is unusual and does not fit into any of the previously presented lines of thought on the Trinity. On it, however, it is once again possible to read the effects of historico-cultural conceptual frameworks on the Christian idea of God.

Erigena was profoundly influenced by the Latin- and Greek-Christian tradition, especially by Neoplatonism. Thus it comes as no surprise that in the attempt to think God and the world together, he taught three phases in which the pure and simple and one God mediates Himself to the world. Differently than in Neoplatonism, however, he sees these three steps less as static-existential quantities; for him they are instead stages in a *process* in which God unfolds Himself into the world: „Becoming is no longer held to be totally incompatible with the concept of God. There thus arises a tendency towards a

---

[399] Cf. by the present author, *Fundamentalchristologie*, loc. cit., pp. 374-384.

dynamism in the image of God that was fully foreign to Erigena's ancient and even Neoplatonic models."[400] This emphasis on dynamism, movement or even on evolution according to the model of an organic development probably has its basis in this Irishman's Celtic mentality, characteristic of which was a progressive organological thinking.

Corresponding to this is also the fact that in his main work, *De divisione naturae (Periphyseon)*, he summarizes all reality, God and the world, under the term *natura*.[401] He divides *natura* into a *first nature*, which „creates and is not created" (*natura quae creat et non creatur*); this is God, the highest and all-exceeding cause, of which we can only know that it is, not what it is. God is such a superior being that he can even be designated as „nothing."[402] This first nature is – in the sense of Neoplatonism – completely one and simple. From it results from all eternity, necessarily and at the same time deliberately, the *second nature*; it is „created and itself creative" (*natura quae creatur et creat*). It is the epitome of the Platonic world of ideas. The ideas are thoughts of God and are themselves the primordial causes (*causae primordiales*) of the visible world. God creates this second nature from Himself, and „descending into the principles of things, he creates, as it were, Himself and begins to be something."[403]

The *third nature* is the visible cosmos which comprises the angel world, men and physical things. It is „created and itself not creative" (*naturae quae creatur et non creat*); in it the *causae primordiales* deploy their activity and appear. The whole process of the self-deployment of God leads to the *fourth nature*, which „neither creates nor is created" (*natura quae nec creat nec creatur*); in it the movement comes to its end and the creation returns to God. God is then all in all and also has a „profit" Himself: He is able to know himself.

Erigena has drawn up a system in which the entire reality is understood as a process of the progressive self-deployment of God, who is its beginning, its middle, and its end („*est igitur principium, medium et finis*").[404] God and creature are in the process not something different, but „one and the same" („*non duo a se ipsis distantia ..., sed unum et id ipsum*").[405] This organological monism is, of course, varied by Christian corrections: the second nature,

---

[400] Ulrich Rudnick, *Das System des Johannes Scottus Eriugena. Eine theologisch-philosophische Studie zu seinem Werk*, (Saarbrücker theologische Forschungen, eds. Gotthold Hasenhüttl and Karl-Heinz Ohlig, Vol. 2), (Frankfurt, Bern, New York, Paris, 1990), p. 167.

[401] Cf. Alois Dempf, *Metaphysik des Mittelalters* (Reprint of Munich and Berlin, 1934), (Darmstadt, 1976), p. 32: „There can scarcely be so complete a scene change as that from the Carthage, Milan or Rome of Augustine to the Ireland and Paris of Erigena, ... to the darkness of *natura naturans* in which Erigena sought God and the world."

[402] *De divisione naturae* 2, 28.

[403] Ibid. 3, 23 (MPL 122, p. 689).

[404] Ibid. 1, 11 (MPL 122, p. 451).

[405] Ibid. 3, 17 (MPL 122, p. 678); cf. also ibid. 2, 2 (MPL 122, p. 528): „Can you deny, for instance, that God and creature are one?"

though necessary, has also, because of the will of God, emerged from Him and there are even implications of free will in connection with the Fall of Man and redemption.

At first it looks very much as if *Erigena*, in consideration of the Christian eschatology, had designed a *quaternity*, not a triadic sequence of steps, to explain God and world/history. This impression is not totally correct, although he himself seems to have been proud of this extension of the Neoplatonic system to include the fourth nature. In reality, however, the Creation, even the creation of Adam, is realized in the second nature, and the third nature, the visible world, has only arisen as a result of the Fall of Man, as a „‚fall' into space and time," which is linked „with the sin of Adam," so that this nature only has a provisional character[406]; its reality, however, is rooted in the second nature. The real („first") creation thus occurs – as in *Origen* – before the beginning of time in the second nature, so that the third only represents a temporary phase whose reality lies in the *causae primordiales* of the second nature and which is only a kind of new physical state of this nature brought about through sin: hence, the third nature becomes „more and more separated out of the system of the four natures."[407] Thus the real and relevant phases of the process are the first, the second – with the third, so to speak, as an appendix – and the fourth nature – again, a triadic system.

Apparently it is the case – something which in fact had already become apparent in the analysis of the early Jewish conceptions and the beginnings of the Christian theology of the Trinity – that under the dominance of specific conceptual frameworks the mediation of God towards the world can only be conceived of in a three-step. This also holds true, with one small variation or complication, for the thinking of *John Scotus Erigena*.

But why did he not simply fall back on the already long established doctrine of the Trinity? Occasionally he does; then he speaks of a connection of Word/Son with the second and of the Spirit with the third nature. *Erigena*, however, also took these allusions back again immediately: after all the Trinity was in the meantime a completely *immanent* „reality" in God and could no longer be classified as belonging to the created domains, in other words, to the economy. This is the reason *Erigena* could not intimately connect Son and Spirit with the economic processes, as was the case in the beginnings of the speculation on the Trinity. They belonged fundamentally only in the first nature, in the one and simple God.

But there the Trinity became aporetic: God is for *Erigena* „one undivided deity" („*una deitas individua*")[408] or „a simple and undivided one" („*simplex et*

---

[406] Tullio Gregory, „Vom Einen zum Vielen. Zur Metaphysik des Johannes Scotus Eriugena," in *Platonismus in der Philosophie des Mittelalters*, ed. W. Beierwaltes (Wege der Forschung, Vol. CXCVII), (Darmstadt, 1969), p. 349.

[407] U. Rudnick, loc. cit., p. 172.

[408] *De divisione naturae* 2, 23 (MPL 122, p. 568).

individuum unum"),⁴⁰⁹ nevertheless, on the basis of the course taken until then by the development of church doctrine, he had to place the Trinity here, in the first nature. „It is thus most likely that Erigena simply took over the doctrine of the Trinity as a part of the Christian concept of God,"⁴¹⁰ without therefore making even the beginnings of an attempt to pluralize the unity of God. The Trinity is a moment of the normative tradition that at the time of *Erigena* was already so bound up in the immanence of God that it could no longer be classified as being part of the progressive stages of the system. He could thus no longer bring the three hypostases into play to explain the reality of the world and its connection with God; it is now always – the naturally in Himself Trinitarian – God Himself who Himself takes effect.

In order to be able to understand the entire reality as *one* process of the self-unfolding of God, he was forced – now outside of the simply adopted Trinitarian tradition – to „reinvent" the Trinity concept in the second/third and the fourth nature. In plain English, under certain cultural conditions, the conception of *Erigena* demonstrates this, the monotheism *must* differentiate itself triadically. Here, too, these *new triads* – parallel to the merely adopted and functionless tradition of the Trinity – prove to be a product of certain contexts in the history of ideas.

The system of *Erigena* was so unusual for its time that it had, strictly speaking, no immediate consequences for the history of the doctrine of the Trinity. Nevertheless, its influence began to show insofar as especially in the medieval Platonic tradition, for example, in the school of Chartres, progressive thinking gains in significance and becomes associated with the Trinity: „The world is the going out of God through the personal-creative positing of His will; its dynamism is the return to the Spirit-God; it is itself a closed-living movement."⁴¹¹ Over and over again, up until the thinking of *G.W.F. Hegel* († 1831) of God as „absolute movement in itself,"⁴¹² correspondences can be found to the approach of the great Irishman of the Carolingian era.

---

⁴⁰⁹ Ibid. 3, 22 (ibid., p. 687).
⁴¹⁰ U. Rudnick, loc. cit., p. 161.
⁴¹¹ Theodor Steinbüchel, *Christliches Mittelalter* (Photographic reproduction of Leipzig, ¹1935), (Darmstadt, 1968), p. 68.
⁴¹² Thus the title given by an editor to one of Hegel's texts in TzT 2.2, No. 166.

8. Nothing New Since the Middle Ages

An intellectual history is never concluded. So, too, has critical reflection on the Trinity to this day experienced an abundance of the most varied, more or less profound, sometimes even original approaches. If it were therefore a question of attempting a general overview of the theology of the Trinity, then the further development would likewise need to be addressed.
That, however, is not the aim of this study. It has merely been to demonstrate how and why the ecclesiastically normative *make-up of the Trinitarian formula* came about. However, its development, in the Eastern churches since the fourth century, in the Western Christian faith since Early and High Scholasticism, has been essentially concluded.
All further theology builds on these foundations; they themselves, however, have remained unexamined, have been taken for granted for all further thought and have then been interpreted, in part on the basis of new formulations of the problems. As far as the interpretations are concerned, they have naturally been conditioned in turn by the given contexts, in particular from the standpoint of soteriological interests. From this, it goes without saying that one broad „Western" line has developed in which the Trinitarian formula, though – duly – reproduced, has, in fact, faded in importance in favor of the One God: *God* created the world, revealed Himself, became a man and redeemed or justified us. In another line, the triple personality – even including the conception of an intradivine community of love – comes to the fore; here the monotheism then becomes problematic.
Yet another situation can be see in the theologies of Africa and Asia that are gradually beginning to take shape and that are adapting the Trinitarian formulas on the basis of totally foreign soteriological traditions and assimilating them into their thinking.
Also playing a role in addition to this are all sorts of influences in the history of ideas, from philosophy up to sociology, and even social developments, such as they are reflected, for example, in liberation theology or in feminist theology. Depending on the circumstances, the Trinitarian formula tradition is appropriated with specific main focuses: the Trinity as a solidary fellowship, the persons as dialogical-relational quantities, the Spirit as „feminine spirit," etc.
All of this is quite interesting and would be worthy of an investigation of its own. However, although it enriches Trinitarian speculations, it cannot substantiate and intellectually secure the phenomenon itself, the Trinitarian dogma. This is why constructs of this sort collapse when the foundation, upon which they are so naturally building, is removed. It is, however, this foundation which has been the concern of this study. Its intention has been to demonstrate how and from what motivations the Son and the Spirit were added to the „Father of Jesus" and the original undifferentiated monotheism was

pluralized into the Trinity. This seems, with the viewpoints cited and the evidence adduced, to have been documented sufficiently enough to make it possible to dispense with a presentation of the later history.

9. From Monotheism to the Intradivine Community of Love

9.1 The Contextual Limitation of the Trinitarian Dogma

Jesus himself stood in the tradition of Jewish monotheism, more exactly, of Palestinian early Judaism. His thinking and acting were geared towards this One God by whom he felt himself to have been sent and to whom he felt close, so that – again following early Jewish practice – he called him Father.

It needs to be explained how and why, from the second century on, this fundamental monotheism underwent a binitarian and Trinitarian „enrichment." This would be relatively simple if the narrative documents of Christianity, above all the soon-to-be-so-called New Testament, had suggested such a doctrinal development. That is however not the case. The New Testament contains at best in a few places the onset of a Hellenistic-Christological thinking in which Jesus appears as divine or even as the incarnated Logos; these passages are thus potential points of departure for a doctrine of the binity. Nothing similar is said of the Spirit. In the vast majority of the New Testament, however, Jesus is God's representative, an eschatological man who after his death was raised to God. The sporadic triadic formulas are by no means to be viewed in the sense of an „implicit" concept of the Trinity.

In the later theology of the Trinity to this day these facts have for the most part been simply overlooked or, if the problem contained therein has once been thematized, have been reinterpreted through interpretive acrobatics. Moreover, this difficulty has been known of for some time. Already in the fourth century *Gregory Nazianzen* wrote: „The Old Testament has clearly proclaimed the Father, the Son (on the other hand) in a way that is hard to understand. The New Testament has revealed the Son and has only intimated the divinity of the Holy Spirit in a concealed way. Now the Spirit is living among us and revealing itself more clearly. When the divinity of the Father was still not acknowledged, it would not have been smart openly to proclaim that of the Son. And when the divinity of the Son was still not accepted, one could not in addition to that – I am speaking much too boldly – saddle (people) with the Holy Spirit."[413]

At any rate, *Gregory*, the authority on the Bible, is aware of the facts of the matter; nevertheless it is still not surprising that he, the theologian of the Trinity, „comes to terms with" the Trinitarian deficits of the Bible in the light of later theology. However, this is more astonishing in contemporary theology, which should have passed through the purgatory of the Enlightenment and of historico-critical thinking, and which produces and is familiar with the exegetical literature and the historical studies on the development of the

---

[413] *Or.* 31, 26 („Fifth Theological Discourse" [German: *Die fünf theologischen Reden*, ed., introd., and trans. Joseph Barbel (Düsseldorf, 1963), p. 263]).

doctrine of the Trinity. Here one also encounters attempts to interpret the New Testament and the tradition from the point of view of the wording of later formulas and thus the failure to take seriously one's own otherwise asserted critical function.

If, however, one gets involved with the historical facts, one is then forced to see that the conceptions of the Trinity began to develop in Christianity only from the 2nd century on, and the „actual" immanent doctrine of the Trinity, only in the 3rd century. Active in the process were cultural mentalities which *had to* give rise – a glance at comparable early Jewish tendencies shows this as well – to this development. In addition to this, there were also more „accidental" factors which shaped the individual aspects of the history of the Trinity.

9.1.1 Cultural-Historical Inevitabilities

The idea of the Trinity is a „further development" of the monotheism that originated in the Jewish religion and was inherited by Christianity. This monotheism had itself developed in a long process in the history of religion. After the adoption of Yahweh from extra-Israelite origins, this God changed from the mountain and volcano god, ancestral god and god of the highways and byways, into the national God of Israel and finally into the universally and solely valid figure. To be sure, Yahweh remained in the process a God of history: he stood at its beginning, exerted supremacy over it and brought about its future – first that of the tribes, then that of the nation, finally – with the emergence of eschatological thinking – of all nations in a new eon and – after the development of the hope of resurrection in early Judaism – even that of the individual faithful and soon of all mankind.

For Yahweh the Hebrew language did not have the generic term „god"; because Yahweh was completely felt to be the historically acting „vis-à-vis," analogous to a person, there was no obvious need to develop such a term. Later, however, there was an equivalent, *Elohim*, which characterized Yahweh as the quintessence of all (Canaanite) *Els*, but was then rendered – as in the Greek translation of the Old Testament – by *théos*, „God."

This Greek translation thus designated Yahweh as belonging to the genus god and, even though He was viewed as the only member of the genus, on the one hand, it was now possible at least theoretically to imagine even more members of this genus and, on the other hand, a distinction had become possible between an „essence" of God and its realization in *one* or in *several* „concretions" (hypostases) – one of the foundations of the later Trinitarian development.

With the concept of god Hellenism connected a series of associations which were then also internalized by the Hellenized Jews: God is the one and final ground of the cosmos and so also of mankind, hence the *immanent principle*; He (or better, *It*) is omnipotent, omniscient, eternal, incapable of acting; He

(It) is one, unchanging and therefore not capable of contact with plurality and mutability.

As has been described, the Hellenization of the Jews in the Diaspora brought a syncretism of monotheism and the Greek concept of god. In their new cultural character, these people „needed" both lines of representation in order to find a „solution" for their way of problematizing the world and history and of posing the question of their meaning.

Yahweh became the supreme, simple and unchanging being which could not itself perform the mediation to the world – in the Creation – and to history – in the economic action of salvation. At the same time, He remained the reality that stood opposite the world – as the totally other in the diastasis of creator and creature – and also for that reason could not Himself become the principle of the creaturely reality, and yet nevertheless sets creation and salvation going.

Thus it was natural or was even imperative to accept under Him and next to Him other hypostases of a divine sort who could perform the economic mediation duties, that is, demiurgy and the action of salvation history. These had to be quite close to Him or themselves divine so that God Himself would remain the one who is behind everything, but they could not be divine in the same (absolute) sense because they had to have an affinity with plurality and with change.

In early Judaism this function was increasingly taken on by Wisdom, by two angels as the „hands of God" or by the Logos, adopted from Hellenistic philosophy and in all probability from the Stoics, the world's most intimately constituting principle. Whatever these hypostases were called and whatever the religious traditions were from which they were taken, they were „needed" *for the explanation of the economy*; basically they represent the hypostatization of the economic functions of God. In the triadic conceptions, *each* of the functions, demiurgy and acting in history, was hypostatized *separately for itself*; in the binitarian conceptions there was only *one* hypostatization of the economic action in general, so that Wisdom or Logos were then responsible *for both aspects*.

In any case, in both variations their existence begins only „in the beginning." *At that time* they were created by God or emerged from Him, whereby there was simultaneously the possibility – at least for Wisdom and the Logos – of taking them up into God Himself beforehand as merely different designations of God (and wherever this was reflected upon – as is the case in *Tertullian* – also of reintegrating them into God after the end of the economy).

As a result of the „re-Palestinization," this thinking had not been resumed since the latter part of the first century, but was then taken up again by the Diaspora Jewish-Christians and all the more so by the „pagan Christians" and was in fact more vehemently championed by the latter, to whom, on the basis of their own tradition, the Jewish and Jesus-related monotheism was foreign. An additional motivation in this direction resulted with the development of a Hellenistic Christology, according to which Jesus as Christ was said to mediate between the world of the infinite and the finite, between God and man, and must therefore belong to both domains. Jesus in this understanding could then only be appropriated as *the* mediator of salvation if he was divine or even the incarnated God.

There were tentative suggestions of this at only a few places in the New Testament, the vast majority of which, despite its having been written by Diaspora Jewish-Christians, has no preexistence Christology. The impulses provided by these passages were in no way so influential that they became, for example, the dominating topic in the literature of the „Apostolic Fathers" or in Syrian Christianity. However, they were picked up by the Hellenistic apologists, polished and combined with the view of God and His Logos existing since *Philo*; a conception of the binity had arisen which in these cultural contexts was inevitable for the purpose of explaining the creation of the world and the redemptive activity of God, especially in Jesus Christ. The Spirit was also occasionally mentioned in passing – here initiated by the (misunderstood) triadic formulas of the New Testament.

The reason that the doctrine of the binity or the Trinity – save initially in the Syrian and in the Latin church – was ultimately able to become established can be traced to the *Hellenistic mentality* at the time of the Roman Empire that articulated itself paradigmatically in Gnosticism, but which had also included Christian-Hellenistic communities in which Gnosticism was able, to a large extent, to gain a foothold. To this way of thinking, it was obvious and natural that there would have to be an abundance of mediating hypostases between the good and simple God of Light and the world formed of evil and matter; otherwise the association of God and world seemed *rationally* unexplainable.

Against this background it was to be expected that Christians also shared this conviction and it should already be viewed as a considerable critical achievement of the theological writers at the end of the second and at the beginning of the third century that they limited the escalation in Gnostic emanations to the number of two hypostases proceeded from God. A critique beyond this was not yet possible at the time; this would have had as a prerequisite the scrutinizing of the conditions of their own thinking in a kind of meta-reflection. Something like that is scarcely possible for contemporaries.

In any case, this reduction to Word and Spirit made it possible for contemporary theologians to reflect on the thinking about God, which they had taken over from the apologists, in terms of its assertions and above all its compatibility with monotheism. *Irenaeus* and especially *Tertullian* now quite bluntly preached an *eternal monotheism*, which, however, had been *since* „the beginning" *extended economically to include Son and Spirit*: For the purposes of world creation and redemption – revelation to the „Fathers," Incarnation in Jesus and sanctification – God needed his „hands" (*Irenaeus*); *the extension of the monotheism to the Trinity is a matter of salvation history* that should not threaten the eternal monotheism.

The next stage in the speculation on the Trinity is also conditioned by the history of culture: the first shifting of the triadic hypostases from salvation history into „God Himself," that is, the creation of an „immanent" conception of the Trinity in the first half of the third century. the requisite intellectual know-how was delivered by Neoplatonism with its three divine gradations – the One (τὸ ἤν), the Spirit (ὁ νοῦς) and the (world-)soul (ἡ ψυχή) – which mediate from the pure and simple One to the diversity of the cosmos, but which themselves belong to the sphere of the divine.

The reflections of *Origen* are to be seen in this context: He recognizes that it is part of the concept of God for Son and Spirit that they do not exist only since „the beginning"; it can be assumed that they are for all eternity with the Father in the divine sphere, although Son and Spirit – this, too, suggested by Neoplatonism – represent lesser forms of the divine, an inner-godly subordinationism. However, since in the tradition Word and Spirit are quite closely connected with their economic functions, *Origen* could not (yet) separate them from them. Here, too, Neoplatonism offered him the pattern. He transposed creation and Christology into the preexistence; the first – purely spiritual creation – as well as the linking of the soul of Jesus with the Logos took place within the divine realm. The second creation and also the Incarnation occurred only on the basis of a likewise prehistoric fall from grace, for the purpose of the purification of souls – this is also a Neoplatonic motif.

Since then, however, there is for the first time an immanent Trinity: God is already triadically structured *before* „the beginning." From now on the discussion proceeded at this new level. *Arius* contributed – unintentionally – to the stabilization of this „quality leap." Like *Origen*, he also thought that eternity is an integral part of real godhood. But from the point of view of his Syrian theological origins he drew the opposite conclusion from this: Thus there is only the one and same God. The Logos which before the Creation did not exist, is for just this reason not God, but creature. That *Arius*, for Christological motives, clung after all to a preexistent Logos which is incarnated in Jesus, stemmed from his consideration of the soteriological interests of his parish in Alexandria. His adversaries, who due to the Council of Nicaea were at first victorious, therefore had to defend the comprehensive godhood of the Son. These objectives led to the denial not only of his temporality, but also of a vesting with less than generic powers, in other words, an intradivine subordinationism; the result was the *homoousios*, the doctrine of the equality of the nature of the Son with the Father.

Now what this really means remained controversial for some time and there were a great variety of interpretations. At the same time, there arose resistance to the naming of the Spirit, which beforehand had only been mentioned in passing in the discussions, at the same level, probably from circles that wanted to protect the monotheism from at least this further complication. *Gregory Nazianzen* still felt after all that, with the Spirit, theology was „saddled" with a kind of burden.[414] The Nicene *homoousios* for the Son, however, now no longer permitted the Spirit named third in the baptismal order to be conceived of as creaturely; and soon it was formally expanded to include the Spirit as well.

The formula proposed by *Basil* of the one *ousía* and the three hypostases or *prósopa* was in this situation a logical conceptual résumé of the state of the discussion. It is the linguistic conclusion and simultaneously the fixing of a complication of Christian monotheism through the influence of Hellenism. In this, history shows that the creation of a concept of the binity was inevitable from the standpoint of cultural history, while the inclusion of the Spirit, although perfectly appropriate, was not absolutely necessary; here the triadic formulas of the New Testament, which were read in a new way, tipped the scales.

The long holding onto monarchianism by the Syrian and the Latin church is in the same way a result of their cultural character. They – for different reasons – did not „need" any being-like hypostatizations of economic functions. In the more historically oriented Syrian tradition, the one God who created the world, spoke to the „Fathers," chose Jesus in a special way and blesses the Christians, „sufficed." The Latin church saw in God more the one lawmaking will that inflicts punishment for the *impietas* of mankind and is reconciled through the death by crucifixion of the righteous Jesus.

But eventually both churches adopted the Greek consensus formula. That, too, is plausible from the point of view of the contexts of the day: If an agreement could be reached in the general church – and it was ecclesiologically required – it was possible only at the level of the dominant Hellenistic-Christian thinking, because even the West Syrians and Latins were Hellenized, although not so profoundly that their own motivations would have been fully superseded. Thus it can be noted, for example, that *Theodore* of Mopsuestia, the most important Syrian theologian, although adopting the language of the Trinitarian and Christological formula, sought to give it a monarchian and probationary Christological sense. And in the same way *Augustine*, despite authoritative acceptance of the definitions passed on from the East, in the question of God placed a very strong emphasis on the idea of the unity and in the Christology on the justification.

As a consequence, it thus turned out that *the Trinitarian complication* of the Jewish monotheism with which Christianity had been provided as a heritage and model is *a product of circumstances in the history of culture and the soteriological needs resulting from them*. Nothing in this history is incomprehensible or a „mystery," not even the, at least in the more discriminating theology, resulting aporias. On the contrary, the latter document the fact that a theologian of that time, though he had no chance of „dropping out" of his normative traditions or of – historico-critically – recognizing their contingency, nevertheless, standing within them, sensitively perceived the

---

[414] Cf. above p. 121-122.

problematic nature of a mediation of unity and trinity and sought to react to it. Then the only time there were no difficulties was when a tradition was monarchian, be it indiscriminately or in a „dynamistic" or „modalistic" interpretation, or when the problem was conceived of in a simplistic tritheistic way.

9.1.2 Two Historical „Accidents" and Their Impact

The adoption of the Eastern development of the Trinity in the Latin West was due, as described, to the historico-cultural consequence of the West's being embedded in the comprehensive Hellenistic culture; it is equally understandable that *within* this conception it at first, and in part also later on, put the main stress on the unity of God.

In addition to that, there are two significant, so to speak, historical „accidents" which finally led to a conception of the Trinity that was both new with respect to the theology in the East and met with opposition there: the history, on the one hand, of the concept of person and, on the other, the doctrine of the Spirit as a „bond of love" as well as of its proceeding from the Father *and from the Son*.

Here, of course, labeling these as „accidental" only applies to the fact *that* these two motifs came into play at all, but not to their further evolution. It was by no means the result of inevitabilities that *Tertullian* introduced the concept of person to characterize both the trinity in God and the point of unity between the divine and human nature of Jesus Christ. For 150 years this term then led a shadowy existence, until *Augustine* took it up once again. Although he did not like it either, it seemed to him to be less objectionable than any of the other Latin equivalents for the Greek word *hypóstasis*. Neither for *Tertullian* nor for *Augustine* did *persona* already have the later connotation in the direction of the individuality of a spiritual existence. But at least by the time of *Augustine* this meaning already seemed to be getting a little closer.[415] Nevertheless, he could still say: „Man (Jesus, K.-H. O.) is added to God and there arises *one* person" („accedit homo deo et fit una persona").[416] The Christological person is thus the *product* of the unification of God – not *verbum* – and man; it is not the eternal *persona* of the *verbum*, which in addition to its divine nature has taken on a human one. „Person" therefore still does not have for him the sense it will have in the definition of *Boethius*, and after all *Augustine* also basically explains it by means of the concept of relation with the intention of not pluralizing God's simple being.

Especially in the course of the Christological discussion after Chalcedon, whose symbol came to be more and more understood in *Cyril*'s interpretation (the so-called neo-Chalcedonism), the search was on for a describable point of unity in

---

[415] Cf. by the present author, *Fundamentalchristologie*, loc. cit., pp. 262-265.
[416] *Sermo* 293, 7 (MPL 38, p. 1332).

Jesus Christ that could *not* be *natural*, since after all according to the symbol of Chalcedon the natures are united „without confusion," although „inseparably." A solution was sought in the East with the help of the notion of *one energeia* (monenergetism), *one* will (monotheletism) or with the help of the doctrine of the *anhypostasia* and *enhypostasia*[417]; Boethius also wanted to describe, using the concept of person, a point of unity that was not natural – the *individua substantia rationa(bi)lis naturae*.

All of these conceptual models thus aim in the same direction. It was also probably for reasons relating to cultural history that in the Latin West it was precisely the person in the sense of individuality that was given priority, since here, after all, one was less fascinated by the general, ideal being and more oriented toward praxis and the concrete. It was no accident that the first autobiography in world literature, the *Confessiones* of *Augustine*, were written in the West.

The definition of *Boethius* was a big success and also became ever more dominant in the theology of the Trinity, so that the notion of *three subjects* each with its own self-consciousness in God was widespread; nevertheless, this schema was from time to time problematized in higher theology by a reference back to the relational terminology of *Augustine*.

Yet even the latter had been altered since the Middle Ages and associated with concrete „contents" through a rashness on the part of *Augustine*, who had taken over a Neoplatonic motif – in neo-Nicene mediation via the Eusebians[418] – of the third hypostasis, the Spirit, as „bond" and as „love" between Father and Son, from out of which the Western *filioque* also resulted.

Among theologians who lacked both the strong concern for the unity of God and an awareness of the problem approaching that of *Augustine*, there arose from this, since the early Scholastics, in connection with the development of the „modern" concept of person, the thesis that there were *in God three subjects joined together in love*. With that, for the first time, that is, from the 12th century on, the Trinity was fully explained immanently, „sufficiently," and even, as it was thought, „necessarily."

9.2 A Religious Studies Résumé and a Theological Question

Viewed from the point of view of religious studies, the doctrine of the Trinity grew out of the syncretism of Judaism and Christianity with Hellenism and the subsequent addition of Jewish and Christian monotheism with Hellenistic monism. God could thus be simultaneously the Christians' addressee analogous to a person to be appealed to by Christians as well as, through the mediation of the Logos, the immanent creative principle and „subject" of revelation, Incarnation and justification. The extension of this „doubling" to the Trinity

---

[417] Cf. above p. 84-85.
[418] Cf. above 6.3.4.

clearly suggested itself from the viewpoint of cultural history, but was essentially the obvious conclusion that one later drew from the triadic formulas of the New Testament, above all, from the baptismal order.

The fitting together of these two opposing conceptions of God was facilitated by the fact that the monotheistic God in Hellenistic Christianity was fully equipped on its own with being-like and genus-appropriate traits which, from the perspective of its origins out of the tradition of Israel, were foreign to it, at the same time, however, the Logos also took on „personal" coloring through its Incarnation in Jesus. This „facilitation," however, also contributed to a situation in which the economic-Trinitarian talk not infrequently came close to a polytheism – a ditheism or tritheism. To counteract this, there had to be a shifting of the second and third hypostasis into God Himself and then the doctrine of the one nature had to be created. As a result the doctrine of the Trinity thus appears to be an *attempt to combine monotheism, monism and polytheism, hence all of the important world-religious and advanced cultural conceptions of God.* The tendency, however, of most of the theologians involved in this enterprise, as is shown by history, was in the process to hold on tight to the monotheism as *the* central aspect of the belief in God, no matter how incompletely this may have been achieved in the individual instances.

Perhaps the fascination of the doctrine of the Trinity can be explained by the fact that it seeks to combine the merits – in a suspenseful way – of all of the conceptions of God that have been mentioned: the warmth and the potential for hope that the monotheism awakens; the rational plausibility of a final immanent principle as well as the communicative and social liveliness of polytheism. *Gregory of Nyssa* was already of the opinion that the doctrine of the Trinity represented „the middle between the two opinions," between polytheism and Jewish monotheism – he probably identified the Hellenistic monism with monotheism: „If we keep the unity of nature from the Jewish doctrine, from that of the pagans, however, merely the differentiation of the persons, so is the godlessness healed on both sides by the appropriate remedy."[419]

What the religious scholar is able simply to state, however, signifies at the same time a question for theology about the legitimacy of such a construct. If it is certain – and there seems to be no getting around this assumption – that Jesus himself knew only of the God of Israel, whom he called Father, and not of his own later „deification," by what right can a doctrine of the Trinity then be *normative*? Ought one not instead understand it as a process of assimilation which was only inevitable and probably also legitimate within the context of that time – since otherwise Christianity was not livable – thus as a contingent, contextual complication of the Jesus-related conception of God?

---

[419] Gregory of Nyssa, *Oratio catechetica magna* III, 2 (German: Gregory of Nyssa, The Large Catechetical Discourse. *Oratio catechetica magna*, introd., trans., and annot. Joseph Barbel [Bibliothek der griechischen Literatur, eds. P. Wirth and Wilh. Gessel, Vol. 1], [Stuttgart, 1971], pp. 36-37).

Is it permissible to select the few New Testament passages that provided an impetus for a later binitarian reflection and on their part introduce quite clearly a new thought, as a lasting standard for Christian thinking about God? How, in other words, can one legitimize doctrinal development that actually first began in the second century, only found in the third century the turn to a – completely new – immanent triadic message, was in the fourth – after a fashion – put in formulas and in turn brought about in the Latin West a variation that was different with regard to the previous history? If one were to base the doctrine of the Trinity on „revelation," must one also be able to say where and at what stage in the world this revelation would occur: through Jesus, through the evidence of the New Testament, through the apologists or even through *Origen* or *Augustine*?

No matter how one interprets the individual steps, it is certain that the doctrine of the Trinity, as it in the end became „dogma" both in the East and – even more so – in the West, possesses no Biblical foundation whatsoever and also has no „continuous succession" (*continuo successio*). The assertion of a reconciliation of the different conceptions of God which would be sought by means of the application of the schema „implicit-explicit" no longer has anything to do with the facts. Mere verbal suggestions – for instance simply that the immanent Trinity simply is the economic Trinity – do not help one get any further. Theology must gradually face the facts.

This conclusion is by no means an arbitrary questioning of binding doctrine, but the result of historical circumstances which simply were not otherwise. The *history* of the doctrine of the Trinity is *for its part* a question addressed to theology as to how it intends to deal with its own norms and with the asserted continuity to what for Christianity are canonical beginnings.

List of Abbreviation

BKV	O. Bardenhewer, Th. Schermann (ab Bd. 35: J. Jellinger) und C. Weyman, Bibliothek der Kirchenväter, Kempten 1911ff.
CCL	Corpus Christianorum, series Latina, Turnhout, Paris 1953ff.
Ed. Fischer	Joseph A. Fischer, Die Apostolischen Väter, griechisch und deutsch, München 1965
Fontes Christiani	Fontes Christiani. Zweisprachige Neuausgabe christlicher Quellentexte aus Altertum und Mittelalter, hrsg. von Norbert Brox, Wilhelm Geerlings, Gisbert Greshake, Rainer Ilgner, Rudolf Schieffer, Freiburg, Basel, Wien, Barcelona, Rom, New York, ab 1991
LThK^2	Lexikon für Theologie und Kirche, hrsg. von J. Höfer und Karl Rahner, 2. Aufl., Freiburg ^{2}1957ff.
MPL	J.P. Migne, Patrologia Latina, Paris 1878-1890
Neuner-Roos	Josef Neuner/Heinrich Roos, Der Glaube der Kirche in den Urkunden der Lehrverkündigung, neu bearbeitet von Karl Rahner und Karl-Heinz Weger, Regensburg ^{10}1979
SCh	Sources Chrétiennes, hrsg. von H. de Lubac und J. Daniélou, Paris 1941ff.
TzT 2,1	Gotteslehre I, bearbeitet von Herbert Vorgrimler (Texte zur Theologie. Dogmatik, 2,1, hrsg. von Wolfgang Beinert), Graz, Wien, Köln 1989
TzT 2,2	Gotteslehre II, bearbeitet von Herbert Vorgrimler (Texte zur Theologie. Dogmatik, 2,2, hrsg. von Wolfgang Beinert), Graz, Wien, Köln 1989
TzT 4,1	Christologie I. Von den Anfängen bis zur Spätantike, bearbeitet von Karl-Heinz Ohlig (Texte zur Theologie. Dogmatik, 4,1, hrsg. von Wolfgang Beinert), Graz, Wien, Köln 1989
TzT 4,2	Christologie II. Vom Mittelalter bis zur Gegenwart, bearbeitet von Karl-Heinz Ohlig (Texte zur Theologie. Dogmatik, 4,2, hrsg. von Wolfgang Beinert), Graz, Wien, Köln 1989
ZThK	Zeitschrift für Theologie und Kirche

Bibliography

References

(Works without specified publication dates are listed above [List of Abbreviation; p. 131])

- Alkuin, Gegen die Häresien des Felix (von Urgel)
- Alkuin, Sieben Bücher gegen Felix von Urgel
- Anselm von Canterbury, Monologion
- Apokalypse des Elchasai, Fragmente (Hennecke-Schneemelcher, Neutestamentliche Apokryphen in deutscher Übersetzung, Bd. II, übers. von Johannes Irmser, Tübingen ^{5}1989, 619-623)
- Apokalypse des Mose (deutsch nach: Riessler, Paul, Altjüdisches Schrifttum außerhalb der Bibel, Heidelberg ^{2}1966, 138-155)
- Aristides von Athen, Apologie
- Arius, Fragmente aus der Thaleia
- Arius, „Die Blasphemien des Arius"
- „Athanasianisches" Glaubensbekenntnis bzw. Symbolum Quicumque
- Athanasius, De decretis Nicaenae synodi
- Athanasius, Erster Brief an Serapion von Thmuis
- Athanasius, Reden gegen die Arianer
- Athenagoras von Athen, Bittschrift für die Christen
- Äthiopisches Henochbuch (Siegbert Uhlig, Das äthiopische Henochbuch. Jüdische Schriften aus hellenistisch-römischer Zeit; Bd. V, Lfg. 6, Gütersloh 1984, 463-780)
- Augustinus, Briefe
- Augustinus, Confessiones. Bekenntnisse. Lateinisch und deutsch. Eingeleitet, übersetzt und erläutert von Joseph Bernhart, München 1955
- Augustinus, De civitate Dei
- Augustinus, De fide et symbolo (Drei Bücher über den Glauben. De fide, übertragen von Carl Johann Perl [Aurelius Augustinus' Werke in deutscher Sprache, hrsg. von C.J. Perl], Paderborn 1968)
- Augustinus, De doctrina christiana
- Augustinus, De trinitate
- Augustinus, Enchiridion ad Laurentium sive de fide et spe et caritate
- Augustinus, Sermones
- Basilius von Cäsarea, Briefe
- Basilius, De spiritu sancto. Über den heiligen Geist, übers. u. eingeleitet von H.J. Sieben (Fontes Christiani, Bd. 12), Freiburg, Basel, Wien, Barcelona, Rom, New York 1993
- Boëthius, Contra Eutychen et Nestorium
- Boëthius, Opuscula Sacra: Ob Vater, Sohn und Geist in substantieller Weise von der Gottheit ausgesagt werden
- Bonaventura, Pilgerbuch der Seele zu Gott

- Cyrill von Jerusalem, Katechesen
- Didache (Apostellehre), Barnabasbrief, Zweiter Klemensbrief, Schrift an Diognet, eingel., hrsg., übertragen u. erläutert von Klaus Wengst (Schriften des Urchristentums, 2. Teil), Darmstadt 1984
- Dionysius Pseudo-Areopagites, De caelesti hierarchia
- Dionysius, röm. Bischof, Fragmente aus einem Brief gegen die Sabellianer
- Eudoxius, Glaubensbekenntnis
- Eusebius von Emesa, Fragmente
- Evangelium der Wahrheit, übers. u. erläutert von Martin Krause u. Kurt Rudolph, in: C. Andresen (Hrsg.), Die Gnosis, 2. Bd.: Koptische und Mandäische Quellen, Zürich, Stuttgart 1971, 63-84
- Gregor von Nazianz, Reden; bes.: Die fünf theologischen Reden, hrsg., eingel. und übers. von Joseph Barbel, Düsseldorf 1963
- Gregor von Nyssa, Das Gebet des Herrn
- Gregor von Nyssa, Reden; bes.: Die große katechetische Rede. Oratio catechetica magna, eingel., übers. u. komment. von Joseph Barbel (Bibliothek der griechischen Literatur, hrsg. von P. Wirth u. Wilh. Gessel, Bd. 1), Stuttgart 1971
- Hieronymus, Epist. 15 ad Damasum
- Himmelfahrt des Jesaja (Hennecke-Schneemelcher, Neutestamentliche Apokryphen in deutscher Übersetzung, Bd. II [übers. von C. Detlef G. Müller] Tübingen ^{5}1989, 562-578)
- Hippolyt, Elenchos
- Hippolyt, Refutatio omnium haeresium, hrsg. von Miroslav Marcovich (Patristische Texte und Studien, hrsg. von K. Aland und P. Mühlenberg, Bd. 25), Berlin, New York 1986
- Hirt des Hermas (Norbert Brox, Der Hirt des Hermas [Kommentar zu den Apostolischen Vätern, hrsg. von N. Brox u.a., 7. Bd.], Göttingen 1991, 75-180)
- Hugo von St. Viktor, De sacramentis christianae fidei
- Ignatius von Antiochien, Briefe
- Irenäus von Lyon. Epideixis, Adversus haereses. Darlegung der Apostolischen Verkündigung. Gegen die Häresien I, übers. u. eingeleitet von Norbert Brox (Fontes Christiani, Bd. 8/1), Freiburg, Basel, Wien u.a. 1993
- Irenäus von Lyon, Adversus haereses. Gegen die Häresien II, übers. u. eingeleitet von Norbert Brox (Fontes Christiani, Bd. 8/2), Freiburg, Basel, Wien u.a. 1993; Adversus haereses. Gegen die Häresien III, übers. u. eingel. von Norbert Brox (Fontes Christiani, Bd. 8/3), Freiburg, Basel, Wien u.a. 1995
- Johannes Scottus Eriugena, De divisione naturae
- Johannes von Damaskus, Genaue Darlegung des orthodoxen Glaubens
- Justin, Dialog mit dem Juden Tryphon
- Justin, Erste Apologie
- Justin, Zweite Apologie

- Kallistus I., röm. Bischof, Fragmente
- Klemens von Alexandrien, Der Pädagoge (Paidagogos)
- Klemens von Alexandrien, Stromata
- Klemensbrief, der Erste (Joseph A. Fischer, Die Apostolischen Väter, eingeleitet, hrsg., übertragen und erläutert von J.A. Fischer, München, Darmstadt ^{1}1956, 1-107)
- Klemensbrief, der Zweite (Didache[Apostellehre], Barnabasbrief, Zweiter Klemensbrief, Schriften an Diognet, hrsg., übertragen und erläutert von Klaus Wengst [Schriften des Urchristentums, 2. Teil], Darmstadt 1984, 205-282)
- Konzil von Frankfurt im Jahr 794
- Laktanz, Divinae institutiones
- Laktanz, Epitome
- Lateransynode von 649, Verurteilung von Irrtümern über die Trinität
- Luther, Martin, Brief an Georg Spenlein (1516)
- Martyrium des Polykarp (Andreas Lindemann, Henning Paulsen, Die Apostolischen Väter: griechisch-deutsche Parallelausgabe, Tübingen 1992)
- Oden Salomos, übers. u. eingeleitet von Michael Lattke (Fontes Christiani, Bd. 19), Freiburg, Basel, Wien u.a. 1995
- Origenes, Adversus Celsum
- Origenes, De principiis
- Origenes, Kommentar zum Römerbrief (Theresia Heither, Origenes: Commentarii in epistulam ad Romanos / Römerbriefkommentar, lateinisch, deutsch [Fontes Christiani; Bd. 2/2], Freiburg im Breisgau u.a. 1992, 30-301)
- Paul von Samosata, Hymenäusbrief
- Paul von Samosata, Synodalbrief
- Petrus Lombardus, Libri IV Sententiarum
- Philon von Alexandrien, Allegorische Erklärung des heiligen Gesetzbuches (Philo von Alexandrien, Die Werke in deutscher Übersetzung, hrsg. von L. Cohn, I. Heinemann, M. Adler u. W. Theiler u.a., Bd. III, Berlin ^{2}1962, 3-166)
- Philon von Alexandrien, Leben Mosis (Philo von Alexandrien, Die Werke in deutscher Übersetzung, hrsg. von L. Cohn u.a., Bd. III, 217-368)
- Philon von Alexandrien, Über Abraham (Philo von Alexandrien, Die Werke in deutscher Übersetzung, hrsg. von L. Cohn, I. Heinemann, M. Adler u. W. Theiler u.a., Bd. I, Berlin ^{2}1962, 93-152)
- Philon von Alexandrien, Über die Cherubim (Philo von Alexandrien, Die Werke in deutscher Übersetzung, hrsg. von L. Cohn u.a., Bd. III, Berlin ^{2}1962, 167-205)
- Philon von Alexandrien, Über die Opfer Abels und Kains, 65 (Philo von Alexandrien, hrsg. von L. Cohn u.a., Bd. III, Berlin ^{2}1962, 207-264)
- Philon von Alexandrien, Über die Träume (Philo von Alexandrien, hrsg. von L. Cohn u.a., Bd. VI, Berlin ^{2}1962, 163-277)

- Philon von Alexandrien, Über die Unveränderlichkeit Gottes, 57 (Philo von Alexandrien, hrsg. von L. Cohn u.a., Bd. IV, Berlin ²1962, 58-110)
- Pistis Sophia (Evangelia infantiae apocrypha. Apocryphe Kindheitsevangelien, übers. u. eingeleitet von Gerhard Schneider (Fontes Christiani, Bd. 18), Freiburg, Basel, Wien u.a. 1995, 325-331)
- Quicumque, Symbol, bzw. „Athanansianum"
- Richard von St. Viktor, De trinitate
- Slawisches Henochbuch (Paul Riessler, Altjüdisches Schrifttum außerhalb der Bibel, Heidelberg ²1967, 452-473)
- Synode von Toledo, die elfte, im Jahre 675
- Tatian der Syrer, Rede an die Hellenen
- Tertullian, Adversus Praxean
- Theodot (2. Jh. n.Chr.), Fragmente
- Theophilos von Antiochien, Ad Autolycum
- Thomas von Aquin, Summa theologica
- Zephyrin, röm. Bischof, Fragmente

Secondary Literature

- Abramowski, Luise, Der Geist als „Band" zwischen Vater und Sohn – ein Theologoumenon der Eusebianer?, in: ZNW 87, 1996, 126-132
- Abramowski, Luise, Zur Trinitätslehre des Thomas von Aquin, in: Zeitschrift für Theologie und Kirche 92, 1995, 466-480
- Adam, Alfred, Lehrbuch der Dogmengeschichte, Bd. 1: Die Zeit der Alten Kirche, Gütersloh ¹1970
- Andresen, Carl, Die Anfänge christlicher Lehrentwicklung, in: ders. (Hrsg.), Handbuch der Dogmen- und Theologiegeschichte, Bd. 1, Göttingen 1982, 1-98
- Balthasar, Hans Urs von, Theologik, Bd. II, Einsiedeln ²1985
- Barbel, Joseph, Zur „Engel-Trinitätslehre" im Urchristentum, in: Theol. Revue 54, 1958, 49-58
- Barth, Karl, Kirchliche Dogmatik, Bd. III/1: Die Lehre von der Schöpfung, Zürich ³1957
- Baus, Karl. Von der Urgemeinde zur frühchristlichen Großkirche (Handbuch der Kirchengeschichte, hrsg. von Hubert Jedin, Bd. 1), Freiburg, Basel, Wien ³1965
- Beck, Heinrich, Triadische Götterordnungen: klassisch-antiker und neuplatonischer Ansatz, in: Theologie und Philosophie 67, 1992, 230-245
- Beyschlag, Karlmann, Grundriß der Dogmengeschichte, Band 1: Gott und die Welt (Grundrisse 2), Darmstadt 1982
- Bibliotheca Trinitariorum. Internationale Bibliographie trinitarischer Literatur. International Trinitarian Literature, hrsg. von Erwin Schadel, Paris, München, New York, Bd. 1: 1984, Bd. 2: 1988

- Boff, Leonardo, Kleine Trinitätslehre (Titel der Originalausgabe „A Santissima Trindade é a melhor communidade, 1988, übers. von Horst Goldstein), Düsseldorf 1990
- Böhlig, Alexander, Gnosis und Synkretismus. Gesammelte Aufsätze zur spätantiken Religionsgeschichte, Teil 1 (Wissenschaftliche Untersuchungen zum Neuen Testament; 47), Tübingen 1989
- Böhlig, Alexander, Triade und Trinität in den Schriften von Nag Hammadi, in: ders., Gnosis und Synkretismus, a.a.O., 289-311
- Bujo, Bénézet, Afrikanische Theologie in ihrem gesellschaftlichen Kontext, Düsseldorf 1986
- Courth, Franz, Trinität in der Schrift und Patristik, Freiburg, Basel, Wien 1980
- D'Sa, Francis X., Gott – Person oder Prinzip? Gottesbegriff im Werden der indischen Theologie, in: Der eine Gott in vielen Kulturen, a.a.O., 169-200
- Dallmayr, Horst, Die großen vier Konzilien. Nizaea, Konstantinopel, Ephesus, Chalkedon, München 1961
- Daniélou, Jean, Trinité et Angelologie dans la théologie judéo-chrétienne, in: Resources de sciences religieuses 45, 1957, 5-41
- Dempf, Alois, Metaphysik des Mittelalters (Nachdruck von München und Berlin 1934), Darmstadt 1976
- Der eine Gott in vielen Kulturen. Inkulturation und christliche Gottesvorstellung, hrsg. von Konrad Hilpert und Karl-Heinz Ohlig, Zürich 1993
- Ebeling, Gerhard, Dogmatik des christlichen Glaubens, Bd. III: Der Glaube an Gott den Vollender der Welt, Tübingen 1979
- Ein Gott allein? JHWH-Verehrung und biblischer Monotheismus im Kontext der israelitischen und altorientalischen Religionsgeschichte, hrsg. von Walter Dietrich und Martin A. Klopfenstein (Orbis biblicus et orientalis, 139), Göttingen, Freiburg/Schweiz 1994
- Flasch, Kurt, Das philosophische Denken im Mittelalter. Von Augustin zu Macchiavelli, Stuttgart 1986
- Gerlitz, Peter, Außerchristliche Einflüsse auf die Entwicklung des christlichen Trinitätsdogmas, Leiden 1963
- Gill, J., Filioque, in: LThK[2], 4, 126-128
- Gnilka, Joachim, Das Matthäusevangelium, 1. Teil: Kommentar zu Kap. 1,1 - 13,58 (Herders Theologischer Kommentar zum Neuen Testament), Freiburg, Basel, Wien 1986
- Gnilka, Joachim, Zum Gottesgedanken in der Jesusüberlieferung, in: Monotheismus und Christologie. Zur Gottesfrage im hellenistischen Judentum und Urchristentum, hrsg. von Hans-Josef Klauck (Quaestiones Disputatae, Bd. 138), Freiburg, Basel, Wien 1992, 144-162
- Gottes ewiger Sohn. Die Präexistenz Christi, hrsg. von Rudolf Laufen, Paderborn, München, Wien, Zürich 1997
- Gregory, Tullio, Vom Einen zum Vielen. Zur Metaphysik des Johannes Scotus Eriugena, in: W. Beierwaltes (Hrsg.), Platonismus in der Philosophie

des Mittelalters (Wege der Forschung, Bd. CXCVII), Darmstadt 1969
- Greshake, Gisbert, Der dreieine Gott. Eine trinitarische Theologie, Freiburg, Basel, Wien 1997
- Grillmeier, Aloys, Jesus Christus im Glauben der Kirche, Bd. 1: Von der Apostolischen Zeit bis zum Konzil von Chalkedon (451), Freiburg, Basel, Wien 1979
- Harnack, Adolf von, Lehrbuch der Dogmengeschichte. Erster Band: Die Entstehung des kirchlichen Dogmas (Unveränd. reprograf. Nachdruck der 4. Auflage, Tübingen 1909), Darmstadt 1964
- Harnack, Adolf von, Lehrbuch der Dogmengeschichte, Zweiter Band: Die Entwicklung des kirchlichen Dogmas I (unveränderter reprographischer Nachdruck der 4. Auflage, Tübingen 1909), Darmstadt 1964
- Hilberath, Bernd Jochen, Der dreieinige Gott und die Gemeinschaft der Menschen. Orientierungen zur christlichen Rede von Gott, Mainz 1990
- Katechismus der Katholischen Kirche, München u. a. 1993
- Katholischer Erwachsenen-Katechismus. Das Glaubensbekenntnis der Kirche, hrsg. von der Deutschen Bischofskonferenz, Kevelaer u. a. 1985
- Kelly, John Norman Davidson, Altchristliche Glaubensbekenntnisse, Geschichte und Theologie, Göttingen 1972
- Koch, Klaus, Monotheismus und Angelologie, in: Ein Gott allein?, a.a.O., 565-581
- Kretschmar, Georg, Studien zur frühchristlichen Trinitätstheologie (Beiträge Historische Theologie; Bd. 21), Tübingen 1956
- Lang, Bernhard, Der monarchische Monotheismus und die Konstellation zweier Götter im Frühjudentum: Ein neuer Versuch über Menschensohn, Sophia und Christologie, in: Ein Gott allein?, a.a.O., 559-564
- Moltmann, Jürgen, In der Geschichte des dreieinigen Gottes. Beiträge zur trinitarischen Theologie, München 1991
- Moltmann, Jürgen, Trinität und Reich Gottes, München 1980
- Monotheismus und Christologie, hrsg. von Hans-Josef Klauck (Quaestiones Disputatae, Bd. 138), Freiburg, Basel, Wien 1992
- Nougier, Louis-René, Die Welt der Höhlenmenschen (franz. Original: „Premiers éveils de l'homme", Paris 1984, übers. von Verena E. Müller), Zürich, München 1989
- Ohlig, Karl-Heinz, Die theologische Begründung des neutestamentlichen Kanons in der alten Kirche, Düsseldorf 1972
- Ohlig, Karl-Heinz, Die Welt ist Gottes Schöpfung. Kosmos und Mensch in Religion, Philosophie und Naturwissenschaften, Mainz 1984
- Ohlig, Karl-Heinz, Ein Gott in drei Personen. Die griechische Komplizierung des jüdischen Monotheismus, in: Gottes ewiger Sohn. Die Präexistenz Christi, hrsg. von Rudolf Laufen, Paderborn, München, Wien, Zürich 1997, 199-226.
- Ohlig, Karl-Heinz, Einer oder drei? Vom „Vater Jesu" zur Trinität, in: imprimatur (29, 1996, 285-291; 340-346; 30, 1997, 8-13; 55-59; 108-111;

147-152; 199-204; 315-323; 31, 1998, 18-27; 74-80; 126-131; 174-180; 219-226)
- Ohlig, Karl-Heinz, Fundamentalchristologie. Im Spannungsfeld von Christentum und Kultur, München 1986
- Ohlig, Karl-Heinz, Spekulation ohne historische Basis, in: imprimatur 30, 1997, 18-21.
- Ohlig, Karl-Heinz, Trinität, in: Lexikon Alte Kulturen, hrsg. von H. Brunner, K. Flessel, F. Hiller u. Meyers Lexikonredaktion, Mannheim, Leipzig, Wien, Zürich 1993, 559.560
- Pannenberg, Wolfhart, Grundzüge der Christologie, Gütersloh ^{5}1976
- Quasten, J., Quicumque, in: LThK^2 8, 937-938
- Radlbeck-Ossmann, Regina, ... in drei Personen. – Der trinitarische Schlüsselbegriff „Person" in den Entwürfen Jürgen Moltmanns und Walter Kaspers (Prof. Dr. W. Beinert zum 60. Geburtstag), in: Catholica 47, 1993, 38-51
- Rahner, Karl, Bemerkungen zum dogmatischen Traktat „De Trinitate", in: Schriften zur Theologie, Bd. IV: Neuere Schriften, Zürich/Einsiedeln/Köln 1960, 103-133
- Rahner, Karl, Der dreifaltige Gott als transzendenter Urgrund der Heilsgeschichte, in: Mysterium Salutis. Grundriß heilsgeschichtlicher Dogmatik, hrsg. von J. Feiner u. M. Löhrer, Bd. II: Die Heilsgeschichte vor Christus, Einsiedeln, Zürich, Köln 1967, 317-401
- Rahner, Karl, Einzigkeit und Dreifaltigkeit Gottes im Gespräch mit dem Islam, in: Schriften zur Theologie, Bd. XIII: Gott und Offenbarung, Zürich/Einsiedeln/Köln 1978, 129-147
- Riessler, Paul, Altjüdisches Schrifttum außerhalb der Bibel, Heidelberg ^{2}1966
- Rudnick, Ulrich, Das System des Johannes Scottus Eriugena. Eine theologisch-philosophische Studie zu seinem Werk (Saarbrücker theologische Forschungen, hrsg. von Gotthold Hasenhüttl und Karl-Heinz Ohlig, Bd. 2), Frankfurt a.M., Bern, New York, Paris 1990
- Scheffczyk, Leo, Lehramtliche Formulierungen und Dogmengeschichte der Trinität, in: Mysterium Salutis, hrsg. von J. Feiner und M. Löhrer, Bd. 2, Einsiedeln, Zürich, Köln ^{1}1967, 146-220
- Schierse, Franz Josef, Die neutestamentliche Trinitätsoffenbarung, in: Mysterium Salutis, Bd. II, a.a.O., 85-131
- Schimanowski, Gottfried, Die frühjüdischen Voraussetzungen der urchristlichen Präexistenzchristologie, in: Gottes ewiger Sohn, a.a.O., 31-55.
- Schnackenburg, Rudolf, Logos, in: LThK^2 6, 1122-1125
- Seeberg, Reinhold, Lehrbuch der Dogmengeschichte, Zweiter Band: Die Dogmenbildung in der alten Kirche (unveränderter reprographischer Nachdruck der 3. Auflage, Leipzig 1923), Darmstadt ^{6}1965
- Steinbüchel, Theodor, Christliches Mittelalter (Reprograph. Nachdruck von Leipzig ^{1}1935), Darmstadt 1968
- Strotmann, Angelika, Mein Vater bist du (Sir 51,10). Zur Bedeutung der

Vaterschaft Gottes in kanonischen und nichtkanonischen frühjüdischen Schriften (Frankfurter Theologische Studien, Bd. 39), Frankfurt/M. 1991
- Tempels, Placide, Bantu-Philosophie. Ontologie einer Ethik (Titel der belgischen Originalausgabe: Bantou-Filosofie, dt. von Joseph Peters), Heidelberg 1956
- Theobald, Michael, Gott, Logos und Pneuma. „Trinitarische" Rede von Gott im Johannesevangelium, in: Monotheismus und Christologie, a.a.O., 41-87
- Urbina, Ignacio Ortiz de, Nizäa und Konstantinopel (Geschichte der ökumenischen Konzilien, hrsg. von Gervais Dumeige und Heinrich Bacht, Bd. I), Mainz 1964
- Werner, Martin, Die Entstehung des christlichen Dogmas, Tübingen ²1941

SAARBRÜCKER THEOLOGISCHE FORSCHUNGEN

Herausgegeben von Gotthold Hasenhüttl und Karl-Heinz Ohlig

Band 1 Wolfgang Pauly: Wahrheit und Konsens. Die Erkenntnistheorie von Jürgen Habermas und ihre theologische Relevanz. 1989.

Band 2 Ulrich Rudnick: Das System des Johannes Scottus Eriugena. Eine theologisch-philosophische Studie zu seinem Werk. 1990.

Band 3 Rüdiger Augst: Lebensverwirklichung und christlicher Glaube. Acedia - Religiöse Gleichgültigkeit als Problem der Spiritualität bei Evagrius Ponticus. 1990.

Band 4 Bernhard Schäfer: Mystisches Erleben im Werk Günter Eichs. Ein Beitrag zur Erforschung der Beziehungen zwischen Mystik und Literatur. 1990.

Band 5 Chong-Sok Choe: Qi, ein religiöses Urwort in China. Von den Knocheninschriften bis zur heutigen Feng-shui-Praxis. 1995.

Band 6 Ulrike Stölting: Zwischen Tradition und Moderne. Eine Analyse der Theologie Dietrich Bonhoeffers unter besonderer Berücksichtigung seiner Christologie. 1998.

Band 7 Ulrich Königstein: Kulturkampf im Bistum Speyer. Eine regionalgeschichtliche Untersuchung. 2000.

Band 8 Karl-Heinz Ohlig: One or Three? From the father of Jesus to the trinity. 2002.